T0366362

Books in the ABICS Publications Series

Badiru, Iswat and Deji Badiru, *Isi Cookbook: Collection of Easy Nigerian Recipes*, iUniverse, Bloomington, Indiana, USA, 2013

Badiru, Deji and Iswat Badiru, *Physics in the Nigerian Kitchen: The Science, the Art, and the Recipes*, iUniverse, Bloomington, Indiana, USA, 2013.

Badiru, Deji, *Physics of Soccer: Using Math and Science to Improve Your Game*, iUniverse, Bloomington, Indiana, USA, 2010.

Badiru, Deji, *Getting things done through project management*, iUniverse, Bloomington, Indiana, USA, 2009.

ABICS Publications

A Division of
AB International Consulting Services (ABICS)

www.ABICSPublications.com

Books for home, work, and leisure

Isi COOKBOOK

COLLECTION OF EASY NIGERIAN RECIPES

ISWAT BADIRU *and* DEJI BADIRU

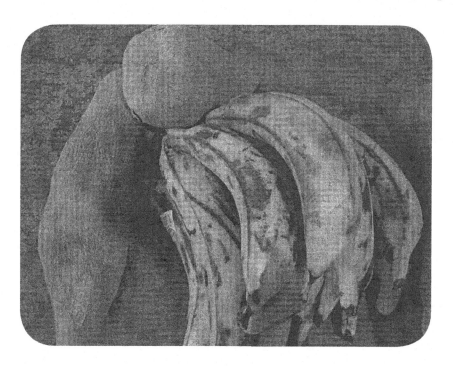

iUniverse, Inc.
Bloomington

ISI COOKBOOK

Collection of Easy Nigerian Recipes

iUniverse books may be ordered through booksellers or by contacting:

iUniverse
1663 Liberty Drive
Bloomington, IN 47403
www.iuniverse.com
1-800-Authors (1-800-288-4677)

Because of the dynamic nature of the Internet, any web addresses or links contained in this book may have changed since publication and may no longer be valid. The views expressed in this work are solely those of the author and do not necessarily reflect the views of the publisher, and the publisher hereby disclaims any responsibility for them.

Any people depicted in stock imagery provided by Thinkstock are models, and such images are being used for illustrative purposes only.

Certain stock imagery © Thinkstock.

ISBN: 978-1-4759-7670-0 (sc)
ISBN: 978-1-4759-7671-7 (e)

Printed in the United States of America

iUniverse rev. date: 2/18/2013

DEDICATION

To Abidemi, Adetokunboh, Omotunji, Deanna, Blake,
and
the memory of our dearly departed parents.

ACKNOWLEDGMENTS

We thank our family and friends for the love and support they have showered on us over the years, particularly during the period of putting together this recipe book.

Iswat Badiru
Deji Badiru
25 December 2012

PREFACE

This book presents a collection of easy-to-prepare Nigerian recipes. Although not a comprehensive coverage of all prevailing recipes in Nigeria, the book presents a representative sample from across the nation.

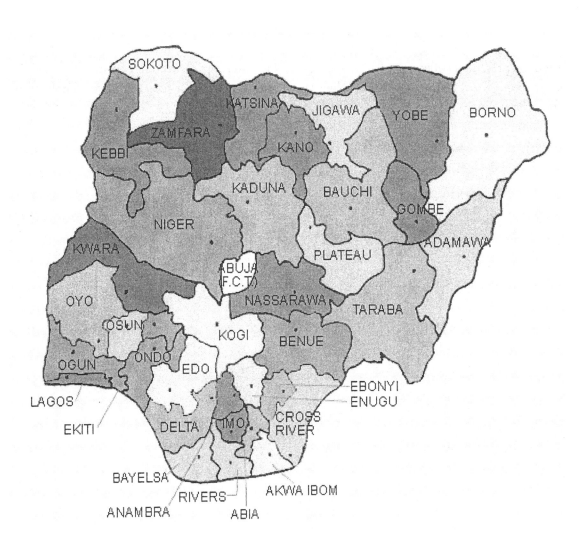

ABOUT NIGERIA

<u>From Wikipedia</u>:

Nigeria, officially the Federal Republic of Nigeria, is a federal constitutional republic comprising 36 states and its Federal Capital Territory, Abuja. The country is located in West Africa and shares land borders with the Republic of Benin in the west, Chad and Cameroon in the east, and Niger in the north. Its coast in the south lies on the Gulf of Guinea on the Atlantic Ocean. The three largest and most influential ethnic groups in Nigeria are the Hausa, Igbo and Yoruba. The name Nigeria was taken from the Niger River running through the country. This name was coined by Flora Shaw, the future wife of Baron Lugard, a British colonial administrator, in the late 19th century. The British colonized Nigeria in the late nineteenth and early twentieth century; setting up administrative structures and law while recognizing traditional chiefs. Nigeria became independent again in 1960. Several years later, it had civil war as Biafra tried to establish independence. Military governments in times of crisis have alternated with democratically elected governments. Nigeria is roughly divided in half between Muslims, concentrated mostly in the north, and Christians, who mostly live in the South. A very small minority practice traditional religions, although the rate of syncretism is high. The people of Nigeria have an extensive history. Archaeological evidence shows that human habitation of the area dates back to at least 9000 BC. The area around the Benue and Cross River is thought to be the original homeland of the Bantu migrants who spread across most of central and southern Africa in waves between the first millennium BC and the second millennium. Nigeria is the most populous country in Africa and the seventh most populous country in the world. Its oil reserves have brought great revenues to the country. It is listed among the "Next Eleven" economies, and is a member of the Commonwealth of Nations.

Source: http://en.wikipedia.org/wiki/Nigeria, accessed Feb 2, 2013

ABOUT NIGERIAN COOKING

Food is celebrated as a key element of the Nigerian culture. Food is embraced for fellowship, worship, and survival. The staple foods of Nigeria include rice, yam, cassava, and wheat (bread). Traditionally, Nigerians (at least the elders) don't cook by recipe. The fine art of cooking Nigerian food is normally handed down through observation, apprenticeship, and experimentation. When asked how they cook so well without a written guide, the older Nigerian mothers would only say that "they just do it." This attests to their experiential learning of the art of Nigerian cooking. As modern practices take root, more and more Nigerians are resorting to the guiding "hands" of written recipes. That is what informs the writing of this book. Our American and European friends often request copies of Nigerian recipes. If not written down, the much-desired Nigerian recipes cannot be disseminatee and promulgated throughout the world. Thus, it is the hope that this book will contribute to providing a lasting archival repository of Nigerian recipes, just as other books before it have done.

Nigerian foods, particularly the soups, are usually spicy hot. Each family often has its own twists and turns to the process of achieving hotter and hotter meals. The common belief is that eating spicy foods is good for the heart and facilitates longevity. "Mild" is not normally in the vocabulary of Nigerian menu, except when dealing with our Western counterparts.

The diversity of thoughts, beliefs, and Nigerian kitchen practices lead to many different ways of preparing the same food. As such, many of the recipes in this book do present alternate approaches to preparing the same basic food. Please don't be timid, experiment and enjoy!

A SAMPLE OF NIGERIAN FRUITS

Eyin (Palm tree fruits)	Mango	Igba (Egg Plant)
Agbalumo/Udara Star Apple	Guava	Cocoa
Pawpaw (Papaya)	Asala (African Walnut)	African Cashew

A SAMPLE OF NIGERIAN VEGETABLES

Shoko	Gbure (Water leaf)	Ewedu
Ora/Oha	Bitter Leaf	Ila (Okra)
Isu (African Yam)	Coco Yam	Casava

TABLE OF CONTENTS

Isi COOKBOOK RECIPES

CHAPTER 1

Breakfast Dishes

Ogi/Akamu/Koko/ (Corn Custard)

Serves 2 - 3

1 cup corn powder

4 cups boiling water

1 cup cold water

Milk or evaporated milk – to taste

Sugar – to taste

PREPARATION

There are two methods:

Method One:
- In a bowl, combine corn powder, sugar, and 1 ½ cup of cold water; mix until the texture is smooth and lump free.
- Pour three (3) cups of boiling water over the mixture slowly. The mixture will rise up as you pour the boiling water; cover for two minutes. For thinner ogi use more boiling water.
- Open and stir Ogi; add more sugar to taste.
- Pour about half (1/2) cup of warm milk or warm water over the Ogi and serve.

Method Two:
- In a deep pot, combine corn powder, sugar, and five (5) cups of cold water; mix until the texture is smooth and lump free.
- Cook mixture at medium high heat; continuously stirring until mixture thickens to avoid lump; reduce heat to low to avoid splashing and cook for five (5) minutes. Add more water for thinner Ogi.
- Pour into a bowl; pour warm milk or warm water over the Ogi; add more sugar and milk to taste.
- Serve with Akara or Moin-moin.

Note: For thicker Ogi use less water and for richer Ogi use milk instead of water for preparation.

Éko (Corn Powder Jelly)

Serves 3

2 cup Ogi (Corn Powder)

10 -10 ½ cups cold water

PREPARATION

- Mix corn powder with five (5) cups of cold water in a deep cooking pot until smooth and lump free then add five (5) more cups of water and stir.
- Cook mixture at medium high heat and stir continuously with a wooden spatula to avoid lumps forming and splashing; continue stirring, mixture will begin to thicken slowly; If lumps are forming, it means the heat is too high, so reduce the heat. When the mixture has completely thickened like Custard, reduce heat to low; add half (½) cup of water, cover and cook for 3-5 minutes. Open and stir thoroughly.
- To check if Eko is done, drop a small amount into some cold water in a bowl, it should sets and floats.
- Dish Eko into small individual bowls and let cool down completely at room temperature or make pouches/pockets with Aluminum Foil, then fill the pouches about 2/3 full; seal the foil at the top by folding several times; cool at room temperature completely.
- Serve with Akara , Moin-Moin, soup or pepper soup.

Akara (Bean Fritters)

Serves many

1 lb. Bag Blackeye Peas or African Red Beans

1 small red bell pepper

1 small to medium onion

2 maggi or knorr cubes – crushed

2 cups of water

Oil or African palm oil – to fry

Salt to taste

PREPARATION

- Clean Blackeye Peas or African Red Beans: See end of the chapter for instruction.

Blending

- Combine cleaned beans, bell pepper, onion and blend. Add water as needed for the blender to rotate; however, do not add too much water or beans will become watery. The beans batter (paste) should be as thick as Pancake batter.
- Pour blended beans into a mixing bowl and mix with a wooden spoon very well to aerate it; add crushed maggi cubes and salt if needed; mix thoroughly until lump free and light.

Frying:

- Deep-fry the mixture by scooping a little amount individually into hot oil and fry until golden. Scoop as many as the frying pan will take. Continue the process until finish.
- Drain on absorbent paper towel in a strainer.

Serve with Ogi, Eko, custard, Quaker Oat, pap or bread.

Moin-Moin (Steamed Beans Cake)

Serves 8 or more

1 lb. bag Blackeye Peas or African Red Beans
1 medium red bell pepper
1 medium onion
4 pieces dry fish (shredded) or one can corned beef
3 - 4 crayfish maggi cubes – crushed
3 - 4 cups of water
½ cup palm oil or canola oil – warm
Salt to taste

PREPARATION

Step 1

- Clean Blackeye Peas or African Red Beans: See end of Chapter for instruction

Blending

- Combine cleaned beans, bell pepper, and onion and blend until mixture becomes a smooth paste. Add water as needed for the blender to rotate. However, do not add too much or beans will become watery. The beans batter (paste) should be a little thinner than Pancake batter.

Step 2

- Make pouches/pockets with aluminum foil or use individual non-stick cupcake cups.
- Shred dry fish and clean in hot water.
- Warm palm oil or oil.
- Pour blended beans into a mixing bowl and mix with a wooden spoon very well to aerate it; add shredded fish or corned beef, crushed maggi cubes and mix; add warm palm oil; salt if needed and mix thoroughly until lump free.
- The beans batter should be a little bite thinner than cake batter.
- Scoop the blended beans into the aluminum pouches one by one; fill half-way to allow room for expansion during cooking. Seal the foil at the top by folding several times.
- Arrange moin-moin into a deep cooking pot and add about 3 - 4 cups of water. Add more if needed.
- Cook for 30 - 45 minutes at medium high.
- Moin-moin is done when it is firm to the touch after exposure to the air for few minutes.
- Unwrap, slice and serve.

Serve with Ogi, Eko, with drinking (soak) Gari, Custard, and Quaker Oat.

Éyin Din-din (Fried Egg)

Serves 3 or more

6 Eggs

Corned beef or sardine – to taste (optional)

1 small onion – diced

1 small red bell pepper – diced

1 large fresh tomato – diced

1 habanera pepper – chopped (optional)

Oil – any type

2 knorr or maggi cubes - crushed

Salt to taste

PREPARATION

On a medium heat sauté onion, red bell pepper and habanera for view minutes; then add tomato, corned beef or sardine and maggi cubes; stir and remove from stove to cool.

In a mixing bowl, beat the eggs then add pepper mixture and mix thoroughly.

Heat oil on a frying pan and fry egg mixture.

Serve with bread, boiled yam or boiled potatoes.

Scotch Eggs

Serves 6

1 dozen eggs

2 - 3lbs. Turkey, chicken, or regular sausage

Breadcrumbs to coat - Finely crushed and seasoned

Flour to coat – Seasoned

4 knorr or maggi cubes - crushed

Ground red pepper to taste - optional

Salt to taste

Oil for frying

PREPARATION

- Boil 6 eggs. Set aside to cool down completely and peel.
- If frozen sausage is used, thaw completely at room temperature.
- Combine the sausage meat with crushed maggi or knorr cubes and mix thoroughly in a bowl.
- Mold sausage meat mixture around the outer layer of each cooked egg one by one.
- In separate bowls, mix three (3) eggs (use more eggs if needed); mix breadcrumbs and flour with some pepper and salt for seasoning.
- Dip each molded egg in the beaten eggs; then roll in the breadcrumbs; then in the flour, if necessary dip back in the mix egg and then in the breadcrumbs once more.
- Deep fry eggs in hot oil until golden and crisp and the sausage meat is completely cooked.
- Carefully remove scotch eggs from the hot oil and drain on absorbent paper towel in a strainer.
- Be careful with hot oil. Do not leave unattended.

Serve whole or slice each one in half for appetizer.

Isu Sisé and Éyin din-din (Boiled Yam with Fried Eggs)

Serves 5 or more

1 large African yam

2-3 cups of water (more if needed)

2-3 tablespoon sugar (adjust to taste) - optional

Salt to taste

6 - 8 eggs

PREPARATION

- Peel the skin off the yam, slice, and wash in cold water.
- Arrange sliced Yam into a cooking pot; add water, sugar and salt.
- Cook until yam is tender (cooked) (20 -25 minutes).
- Remove from heat, drain any left over water; set aside.
- Fry eggs any way and serve over yam.

Serve with fried eggs, stew, enjoy plan with butter, margarine or palm oil.

Isu Din-din/Dun-dun (Fried Yam)

Serves many

1 large African yam

Salt to taste

Hot red ground pepper – optional

Oil

PREPARATION:

- Peel the skin off the yam; slice and wash in cold water.
- Drain and dry sliced yam with paper towel or air dry.
- Sprinkle with salt and pepper to taste.
- Deep fry in any oil or palm oil until golden brown.
- Drain on absorbent paper towel in the strainer.

Serve with fried stew, fried eggs or enjoy plain with butter or margarine.

Dodo ati Éyin Din-din (Fried Plantain with Fried Eggs)

Serves 4 to 6

6 pieces of ripped plantain

Salt to taste

Oil (any type) or palm oil

6-8 eggs

PREPARATION:

- Slice or dice the plantain into pieces; add salt to taste.
- Pour palm oil or oil into a deep fryer or frying pan over medium high heat until hot.
- Place some cut plantain into the hot oil and fry until golden brown.
- Remove from the oil or palm oil and continue the process until finish.
- Drain on absorbent paper towel in the strainer.
- Fry eggs; place dodo on a flat plate and top with fried eggs. Serve hot.

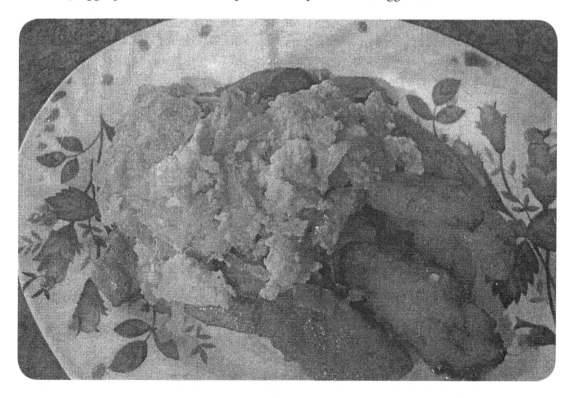

Buns (Nigerian Donuts)

Serves 25 and up

½ bag 5 lbs. All-purpose flour

1 ½ - 2 cups of sugar or adjust to taste

6 large eggs

1 cup butter

1 teaspoon salt

9 - 10 tablespoon water

PREPARATION:

- In a large mixing bowl add flour and knead in butter; add sugar and salt.
- Add eggs and knead; add water little by little and knead into dropping consistency.

Frying:

- Add oil to a deep fryer and heat. Test the oil by dropping a little batter into the hot oil; batter should float to the top.
- Roll batter into individual balls (determine the size) and gently drop into the hot oil or batter can be scooped up by forming a scoop with your hand and scoop up the batter and gently drop into the hot oil. Please be careful with this method.
- Deep fry until light brown or golden brown. Make sure buns are fried through to the inner part. Remove and drain excess oil.
- Serve hot. Okay to warm in the microwave oven.

Puff-Puff (Nigerian Donuts)

Serves 25 and up

½ bag 5 lbs. All-purpose flour
2 cups of sugar or adjust to taste
2 sachets quick-rising yeast
1 tsp. salt
7-8 cups of very warm water

PREPARATION:

- In a large bowl, combine flour, sugar, yeast, salt and mix.
- Add very warm water slowly and mix until desire softness or thickness and lumps free with hand.
- Cover mixed batter and set aside to rise for about three to four hours in a warm or hot spot in the house or outside in the sun. Batter can be mixed and set aside to rise over night also.

Frying:
- Add oil into a deep fryer and heat. Test the oil by dropping a little batter into the hot oil; batter should float to the top.
- Use a scooper, 1/8 of a cup size, or 1/4 of a cup size to scoop up the batter and gently drop into the hot oil to form a ball.
- Also batter can be scooped up by forming a scoop with your hand and scoop up the batter and gently drop into the hot oil. Please be careful with this method.
- Deep fry until light brown or golden brown.
- Continue this process until the batter is finished.
- Optional: Sprinkle puff-puff with powdered sugar.

Serve hot. Okay to warm in the microwave oven.

Meat Pie

Make 25 pies or more (depends on the size)

Meat Mixture:
1 ib. ground beef or turkey
1 ib. ground turkey sausage
2 medium peel potatoes – diced
1 10¾ oz. can Cream of Mushroom Condensed Soup
1 medium onion – chopped
1 medium red bell pepper – chopped
1 medium green bell pepper – chopped
1 habanera or hot chili pepper – chopped
Garlic - to taste – chopped
Curry Powder – to taste
½ cup Milk
2 - 3 knorr or maggi cubes
Salt to taste

When making meat pies, it is best to start with the pastry dough first. The Dough needs to rest for about 3-4 hours before use; unless refrigerated pie crusts are used.

PREPARATION: MEAT MIXTURE

- Sauté diced potatoes for about 5 minutes; then add chopped onion, bell peppers, habanera or hot chili pepper, garlic, ginger, curry powder and maggi or knorr cubes then add milk. Stir and simmer for view minutes then add Cream of Mushroom soup; stir and simmer for view more minutes; set aside to cool.
- Brown ground beef and turkey sausage in a skillet; stirring to crumble the meat (drain any excess fat). Add pepper mixture and mix thoroughly. Set aside to cool. This gives the meat mixture to soak up any juice.

Dough mixture:
5 cups All-purpose flour
2 ½ cups unsalted butter or margarine – cubed and keep cold
4 egg yolks
8 tablespoon cold water
3 tablespoon sugar - optional
Egg white for brushing

Direction:

- Combine flour and butter in a mixing bowl and knead; then add egg yolks, sugar, and knead the dough.
- Then, add the cold water gradually little by little into the dough to form soft but firm dough.
- Roll dough into a ball and wrap with a clear plastic wrap; let it rest for about four (4) hours in the fridge.
- The number of pies from the dough will depend on the size of the pies.
- Roll out some dough, about 1/4 inch in thickness. Don't make it too thick.
- Take a round object, place it on the dough and cut a circle out; then add one tablespoon of the meat mixture in the center of the dough.
- Then fold the dough over the meat mixture and pinch the edges together using a fork so the filling is sealed. Repeat the above steps until out of dough or meat mixture.
- Arrange meat pies on a baking tray (spray or grease the tray).
- In a separate bowl, mix some egg white and brush the exterior of the meat pies before baking.
- Bake at 350 for 25 minutes or until brown or golden brown.
- Serve hot or cool.

Serve with Orange juice, Milk, Tea or coffee.

Sausage Rolls

Make about 8 (depends on the size)

1 ib. Turkey sausage or sausage of choice

1 small onion – finely chopped

1 large carrot – peeled and grated

Some ginger to taste

Some garlic to taste

2 medium eggs

Some milk to brush the sausage roll

½ tsp. ground black pepper

1-2 maggi or knorr cubes

PREPARATION

- Combine sausage, onion, carrot, ginger, garlic, black pepper, maggi cubes and eggs in a large bowl and mix thoroughly.
- Divide sausage mixture into four (4) and roll out to about four (4) inches long each.
- To make dough see (Meat Pie Section) or use readymade dough from store.
- Place rolled sausage on one end edge of dough and roll up to enclose mixture; then cut into 2 pieces each.
- Arrange sausage rolls on a tray (oil the tray first); place seam side down.
- Brush sausage rolls top with milk.
- Bake for 20 – 25 minutes or until golden brown.
- Cool and serve.

Serve with Orange juice, Milk, Tea or coffee.

How to Clean Blackeye Peas or African Red Beans

- Soak blackeye peas in cold water for about five minutes. (This will allow the beans to swell up and make it easy to remove the outer coat); or pour small amount of the beans into the blender, cover with water; grind for about 3 – 5 seconds (do not blend) and pour the beans into a large bowl; continue the process until finish.
- Cover beans with water; rub beans inbetween palms of both hands back and forth in the water to lose the outer coat. The outer coat will naturally float to the top.
- Use a strainer to separate beans from the outer coat by draining the floating coats. Continue this process until beans is cleaned and no more coats or dark sport. Filter and change water as many times as needed.

CHAPTER 2

Lunch or Dinner Dishes:
Okele (Solids) – Eba, Amala, Iyan, Fufu and Semolina

Serve with any Soup or Stew in the Book

Éba – Mashed Cassava Grit

Serves 2 or more

4 cups of water

2 cups of Gari

PREPARATION

- Boil water in a deep pot.
- Remove one cup of the boiling water and set aside for later use.
- Reduce the heat to medium heat to avoid splashing.
- Using a wooden spoon, stir Gari slowly into the water.
- Stir to break up lumps until a smooth consistency is obtained.
- Add remaining hot water only if needed to get softer Eba. Then dish out.
- Because Gari is a little coarse, the resulting Eba will be a little coarse. Filter Gari to make the Eba less coarse and smooth.

Serve Eba with any vegetable soups, okra soup, egusi soup, or ewedu and stew.

Amala – Mashed Yam Flour

Serves 2 or more

5 cups of water

2 cups of Amala flour

PREPARATION

- Boil water in a deep pot.
- Remove one cup of the boiling water and set aside for later use.
- Reduce the heat to medium heat to avoid splashing.
- Using a wooden spoon, add Elubo into the water and stir continuously to break up lumps until a smooth consistency is obtained.
- Add remaining hot water as needed slowly for softer Amala.
- Cover the pot and cook slowly for five (5) minutes, then stir thoroughly and dish out.

Serve Amala hot with any vegetable soup, okra soup, egusi soup, or ewedu and stew.

Iyan – Pounded Yam

Serves 2 or more

5 cups of water

2 cups of Iyan flour

PREPARATION

- Boil water in a deep pot.
- Remove one cup of the boiling water and set aside for later use.
- Reduce the heat to medium heat to avoid splashing.
- Using a wooden spoon, stir Iyan slowly into the water and continue mixing.
- Stir thoroughly to break up lumps until a smooth consistency is obtained.
- Add remaining hot water slowly as needed for softer pounded yam.
- Cook Iyan slowly for five (5) minutes more, then stir thoroughly and dish out.

Serve Iyan with any vegetable soups, okra soup, egusi soup, or ewedu and stew.

Iyan – Pounded Yam (from Fresh Yam)

Serves 4 or more

1 large Fresh Yam

Water

Mortar and Pestle or any substitute

PREPARATION

- Peel the skin off the yam and rinse in cold water.
- Slice or cut the yam into pieces.
- Arrange sliced yam into a deep cooking pot and add water to cover the yam then cook yam until very soft.
- Remove yam from heat; drain left over water and set aside.
- Place small amount of yam in the mortar and pound with the pestle, add more yam and pound; continue until no more yam left.
- Continue pounding until you get firm softer dough with the same consistency.
- Add the set aside water or warm water as needed for softer Iyan or to your like.

Serve Iyan with any vegetable soups, okra soup, egusi soup, Agbono, or awedu and stew.

Semolina

Serves 2 or more

5 cups of water

2 cups of Semolina

PREPARATION

- Boil water in a deep pot.
- Remove one cup of the boiling water and set aside for later use.
- Reduce the heat to medium heat to avoid splashing.
- Using a wooden spoon, stir Semolina slowly into the water and stir.
- Stir well to break up lumps until a smooth consistency is obtained.
- Add remaining hot water slowly as needed to get the right consistency and softer Semolina.
- Stir thoroughly then dish out.

Serve Semolina with any vegetable soups, okra soup, egusi soup, Agbono, or ewedu and stew.

CHAPTER 3

Lunch or Dinner Dishes: Soup and Stew

Serve with Okele (Solids) – Eba, Amala, Iyan, Fufu and Semolina

Obe Ata (Pepper Stew)

This Nigerian stew is a unique blend of tomatoes, onion, fresh hot red pepper, ginger, garlic, seasoning and oil or palm oil.

Serves many

2 lbs. assorted meat – cube (See list & cooking direction at the end of the chapter)
2 15¼ oz. can tomato sauce
1 6oz. can tomato paste
1 large onion
Fresh Ginger – to your taste
Fresh Garlic – to your taste
3 habanera peppers (hot, adjust to taste)
2 red bell peppers
4 maggi or knorr cubes
½ cup oil – less if prefer
Water
Salt to taste

PREPARATION

- Blend tomato sauce, paste, onion, ginger, garlic, habanera peppers and red bell peppers together; add water as needed for the blender to rotate and blend until smooth. Set aside.
- Boil assorted meat: See list & cooking direction at the end of the chapter.
- In a deep cooking pot, combine blended tomato/pepper mixture; maggi or knorr and cook for 20 minutes. Stir occasionally during cooking to avoid burning the sauce. Add ½ to one cup of water if mixture appears too thick and cook for five (5) minutes.
- Add cooked assorted meat; stir and cook for 15 minutes.
- Add oil, cover and cook at low to medium heat for 15 – 20 minutes. Stir occasionally during cooking to allow ingredients to mix evenly.
- Add salt to taste as needed.

Serve over rice or any of the soups in this book.

Note: If cooking fish, do not boil the fish; clean and cut into pieces, sprinkle with little salt and set aside for 30 minutes to marinate before cooking. Instead of stirring soup, lift the pot and shake the pot to mix the contents.

Obe Ata Din-din (Fried Pepper Stew) without Meat

Serves many

2 15¼oz. can tomato sauce
1 6oz. can tomato paste
1 large onion
Fresh Ginger – to your taste
Fresh Garlic – to your taste
3 habanera peppers (hot, adjust to taste)
2 red bell peppers
4 maggi or knorr cubes
Curry powder to taste
Ground thyme to taste
2-3 cups of Oil or more
Salt to taste

PREPARATION

If adding fish to the Fried Stew:

- Clean and cut fresh fish into cubes; season with salt and set aside in a strainer for about 20-30 minutes for the water to drain and marinate then fry and Set aside.

If adding meat to the Fried Stew:

- Cut into pieces boil with any meat seasoning until tender. Add little water as most meat produces water as it cooks. Remove from the pot and put in a strainer to drain any juice from the meat then fry and set aside.
- Blend tomato sauce, paste, onion, ginger, garlic, habanera peppers, and red bell peppers together; add very little water during blending but enough for the blade to rotate.
- In a deep cooking pot, add mixture of blended tomato/pepper, maggi or knorr, thyme and curry. Cover and cook for 30 - 45 minutes at mid heat or until fairly reduced to thick paste; stir occasionally during cooking to prevent burning; reduce heat if necessary.
- Add leftover oil from frying the meat or fish; stir and cook for another 10 minutes. The oil will float to the top. However, if oil is not floating on top, continue cooking at a low heat on cover so that the sauce will become condense lowly and the oil will float to the top. Fried stew takes a lot of oil! So add more if needed.
- Add fried meat, snail or fried fish and stir. At a low heat, simmer for another 10 - 15 minutes.
- Add salt if needed to taste.

Serve over rice, beans or any of the soups in this book.

Ewedu (Jute Leaf) Soup

Serves many

3 cups Fresh Ewedu leaves or one bag frozen – minced

1½ - 2 cups of water

1 tablespoon ground crayfish

1 piece dried fish – shredded

2 tablespoon Egusi (melon) - optional

1 tablespoon Locust beans - optional

1 – 2 maggi or knorr cubes

Salt to taste

PREPARATION

- Remove ewedu leaves from the stem; wash very well in cold water to remove grits; drain and air dry.
- Finely chop up ewedu or grate with little water in a blender (do not blend) and set aside.
- Shred and clean dried fish in hot water; set aside.
- Add two cups of water into a small cooking pot; add dried fish, maggi and cook for five (5) minutes; then add Egusi (melon) and cook for 10 minutes.
- Reduce heat and add Ewedu and mix; add ground crayfish, locust beans, and cook for 5-10 minutes.
- Add salt and more water if needed for thinner ewedu.
- Cook for 2-3 minutes.

Serve with Obe Ata (Pepper Stew) and eat with Amala, Eba, Fufu, Semolina or Iyan.

Obe Ila (Okra Soup)

Serves 4 or more

1 16oz. bag frozen Okra – Finely chopped

2 - 3 cups of water

1 dried fish – shredded (optional)

1 tablespoon ground crayfish (optional)

1- 2 maggi or knorr cubes

Salt to taste

PREPARATION

- Finely chop up Okra and set aside.
- In a cooking pot, add two (2) cups of water, maggi or knorr cubes, dried fish and cook for ten (10) minutes.
- Add chopped okra, ground crayfish, stir and cook for five (5) minutes.
- Add more water if Okra appears thick and cook for view more minutes; add salt if needed.

Server with Obe Ata and eat with Amala, Eba, Fufu, Semolina or Iyan.

Okra Soup with Meat

Serves many

1 16oz. bag frozen Okra - chopped

1 small size stockfish - sliced

1lb. assorted meat – cube (see list & cooking direction at the end of the chapter)

1 tablespoon ground crayfish

½ tablespoon ground hot red pepper

1 tablespoon bitter leaf

½ cup palm oil or 1/3 cup of oil – increase amount to taste

4 maggi or knorr cubes

Water

Salt to taste

PREPARATION

Step 1.

- Chop up Okra (not blend) and set aside.
- Boil sliced stockfish. Cover with water, add some salt and boil until tender; set aside.
- Boil assorted meat: see list & how to at the end of the chapter. Then,
- Reduce heat to medium and add stockfish to meat mixture and cook together for view minutes.

Step 2.

- If there is enough stock in the meat mixture or add 2 – 3 cups of water if needed, add ground red pepper, maggi or knorr cubes and cook for ten minutes. Reduce heat if needed. Add bitter leaf, ground crayfish, mix thoroughly and cook for five (5) minutes; add palm oil, mix and cook for another 10 minutes. Mix occasionally to prevent burning.
- Add chopped Okra and cook for five (5) minutes uncovered.
- Add more water if soup appears too thick little by little to taste; cook for another 2-3 minutes. Stir occasionally during cooking to allow ingredients to mix evenly.

Serve with Amala, Iyan, Eba, Semolina or Fufu.

Bitter Leaf Soup

Bitter leaf soup is a soup prepared with the freshly washed Bitter Leaves. This soup is popularly eaten by the Igbos from Eastern part of Nigeria.

Serves many

12 oz. bag bitter leaf
1 ½ lbs. assorted meat – cubed (see list & cooking direction at the end of the chapter)
1 small stockfish – chopped
2 pieces dried fish – shredded
2 tablespoon ground crayfish
1 small onion - chopped
½ tablespoon ground hot red pepper (adjust to taste)
½ - 1 cup palm oil
4 maggi or knorr cubes
Water
Salt to taste

PREPARATION

Step 1.
- Wash bitter leaves very well to remove most of the bitterness; then soak for about 20 minutes in salted water; drain and set aside.
- Shred dried fish into small pieces and clean in hot water. Set aside.
- Boil sliced stockfish. Cover with water, add some salt and boil until tender; set aside.
- Boil assorted meat. See list & how to at the end of the chapter. Then, add boiled stockfish, dried fish, pepper, onion, maggi or knorr, stir and simmer for ten (10) minutes. Keep stock (broth) in it and reduce heat to low to get bitter leaves ready.

Step 2.
- Add clean bitter leaves into the meat mixture and cook for 10 – 15 minutes. Then add ground crayfish, palm oil to meat mixture and cook for another 15 minutes at medium heat. Occasionally stir soup to prevent burning and also to allow ingredients to mix evenly.
- If soup appears thick, add water little by little until desired thickness is reached.
- Use thickener like cooked cocoyam paste if soup appears watery.
- Salt as needed to taste. Then cook for 5 -10 minutes.

Serve soup with Eba, Amala, Iyan, Semolina or Fufu.

There are different variations of this soup; especially the type of meats, fish or sea food selection.

Some add cocoyam as a source of thickener to the soup.

Apon/Ogbono Soup

Just like Egusi soup, Apon/Ogbono soup is enjoyed by all Nigerians.

Serves many

¼ cup ground Apon/ Ogbono
1 small stockfish – cut or shredded
Some pieces of assorted meat – diced
1 tablespoon ground crayfish (optional)
½ tablespoon ground hot red pepper – or to taste
¼ cup of palm oil or oil
2 - 3 maggi or knorr cubes
Water
Salt to taste

PREPARATION

Step 1.

- Boil sliced stockfish. Cover with water, add some salt and boil until tender; set aside.
- Boil assorted meat: See list & cooking direction at the end of the chapter. Then, reduce heat to medium and add boiled stockfish, cook for view minutes together. Add pepper, ground crayfish, maggi or knorr cubes, and water if needed; cook for 10 minutes and reduce heat to low to get Ogbono read.

Step 2.

- In another pot, add ¼ cup of palm oil and heat; reduce heat; stir in Apon/Ogbono slowly and whisk constantly. Ogbono will rise up and draw as you stir; reduce heat if necessary.
- Gradually stir in 2-3 cups of water and continuously stirring until a smooth consistency is obtained and lump free. Cook for about 10 - 15 minutes at medium heat.
- Pour meat/stockfish mixture into Ogbono; mix, cover and cook for another ten minutes. Stir occasionally during cooking to prevent burning and also to allow ingredients to mix evenly.
- Add more water if soup appears too thick little by little until desired thickness is reached and simmer for another 10 minutes.

Ogbono Soup with Okra – Add two (2) cups of chopped Okra and some water to the soup at the end and cook for 5-10 minutes.

Serve soup with Eba, Amala, Iyan, Semolina or Fufu.

Efo-Riro (Plain Vegetable Soup)

Serves many

2 16oz. bag chopped frozen spinach
1 small size stockfish – chopped
2 pieces smoked or dried fish - shredded
1 tablespoon ground crayfish – optional
3 tablespoon locust beans (Iru)
1 15¼ oz. can tomato sauce
2 - 3 tablespoon tomato paste
1 medium onion
Fresh Ginger – to taste
Fresh Garlic – to taste
3 habanera peppers (hot; adjust to taste)
1 red bell pepper
4 maggi or knorr cubes
½ -1 cup palm oil or 1/3 cup of oil
Water
Salt to taste

PREPARATION

Step 1.:
- Boil stockfish. Cover with water, add some salt & boil until tender; then set aside.
- Soak vegetable in salted water for 20 minutes; drain and remove excess water; set aside.
- Shred dried fish into small pieces and clean in hot water then soak in salted water for about twenty (20) minutes.
- Blend tomato sauce, paste, onion, ginger, garlic, habanera peppers, and red bell peppers; add little water during blending but enough for the blade to rotate; pour into a deep cooking pot and cook on a medium high.

Step 2.
- Add stockfish and smoked fish into tomato mixture and cook for fifteen (15) minutes; then add maggi or knorr cubes, crayfish; mix and cook for ten (10) minutes; mix occasionally to avoid burning.
- Reduce heat; add locust beans, palm oil and cook for ten (10) minutes. At this point, if soup appears watery cook soup longer.
- Add vegetable; mix thoroughly and simmer for another 5-10 minutes; stir occasionally.
- Salt if needed to taste.

Serve soup with Eba, Amala, Iyan, Semolina or Fufu.

Egusi (Melon) Soup

Egusi soup is a popular Nigerian soup. Cooking techniques maybe different from region to region.

Serves many

1 cup ground Egusi
1 small size stockfish – chopped or diced
1 to 1½ lbs assorted meat – See list & cooking direction at the end of the chapter
2 pieces smoked or dried fish (optional) - shredded
2 tablespoon ground crayfish
1 15¼oz. can tomato sauce
2 - 3 tablespoon tomato paste
1 medium onion
1 red bell pepper
2 habanera peppers (hot, adjust to taste)
Ginger to taste
4 maggi or knorr cubes
½ cup palm oil or 1/3 cup oil
Water
Salt to taste

PREPARATION
Step 1.
- Boil stockfish. Cover with water, add some salt and boil until tender; set aside.
- Shred dried fish into small pieces and clean in hot water. Soak in salted water for about 10 minutes and set aside.
- Blend tomato sauce, paste, onion, habaneras peppers ginger, and red bell peppers. Add water as needed for the blender to rotate and blend until smooth. Set aside.
- Boil assorted meat. See list & cooking direction at the end of the chapter. Then, reduce heat to medium; add cooked stockfish, smoked fish and simmer together for view minutes.
- Add tomato/pepper mixture, maggi or knorr cubes; mix and cook for 15 - 20 minutes.
- Add 2 cups of water if soup appears too thick or as needed little by little. Stir occasionally during cooking to avoid burning and to mix ingredients evenly.
- Now, add some broth from the soup into Egusi and mix in. Roll Egusi into tiny little balls and drop or sprinkle each one into the meat mixture; cover and cook for ten (10) minutes at medium heat; then open and stir. Add crayfish and palm oil; cover and cook for 10 minutes; open and stir; then simmer for ten (10) minutes at low heat.
- Add salt and water as needed and cook for 5 minutes at low heat.

Serve soup with Eba, Amala, Iyan, Semolina or Fufu.

Egusi (Melon) and Vegetable Soup

Serves many

1 ½ cup ground Egusi
2 16 oz bag chopped frozen spinach
1 small size stockfish – chopped or diced
1½ lbs. assorted meat – cut or diced (See list & cooking direction at the end of the chapter)
1 tablespoon ground crayfish
1 15¼ oz. can tomato sauce
2 tablespoon tomato paste
1 medium onion
Fresh Ginger – to your taste
Fresh Garlic – to your taste
3 habanera peppers (hot; adjust to taste)
1 red bell pepper
4 maggi or knorr cubes
½ -1 cup palm oil or 1/3 cup of oil
Water
Salt to taste

PREPARATION

Step 1.:

- Soak vegetable in salted water for 20 minutes; drain and remove excess water; set aside.
- Boil stockfish. Cover with water, add some salt & boil until tender; then set aside.
- Shred dried fish into small pieces and clean in hot water; then soak in salted water for about 10 minutes. Set aside.
- Blend tomato sauce, paste, onion, ginger, garlic, habanera peppers, and red bell peppers; add little water during blending but enough for the blade to rotate. Set aside.

Step 2.:

- Boil assorted meat. See list & cooking direction at the end of the chapter. Then, reduce heat to medium; add boiled stockfish and smoked fish; simmer for view minutes together.
- Add tomato/pepper mixture, maggi or knorr cubes; mix and cook for 10-15 minutes; mix occasionally to avoid burning and to mix ingredients together. Add some water if soup appears thick.
- Add some broth from the soup into Egusi and mix in; then roll Egusi into tiny little balls and drop or sprinkle each one into the soup; cover and cook for ten (10) minutes; occasionally stir to prevent burning.
- Add crayfish and palm oil; cover and cook for 10 minutes or until desired thickness is reached. Add vegetable; stir and simmer for another 5-10 minutes; stir occasionally.
- Salt if needed to taste.

Serve soup with Eba, Amala, Iyan, Semolina or Fufu.

Abak Atama Soup

This rich palm nut soup is spiced and flavored with Atama leaves. Atama leaf can be used dried or fresh; the dried leaves are a lot more pungent in flavor.

Serves many

80 -100 bangas (fresh palm kernel seeds) or one can Trofia

8oz. dried Atama leaves – washed and shredded

1 small stockfish – chopped

1-1 ½ lbs. assorted meat - cut or cubes (See list & cooking direction at the end of the chapter)

2 pieces smoked fish - shredded

1 cup Fresh shrimps

8oz. Periwinkle

2 tablespoon ground crayfish

1 medium onion

1 small Uyayak – local spice

1 tablespoon ground chili pepper (hot, adjust to taste)

4 maggi or knorr cubes

Water

Salt to taste

PREPARATION

Step 1.

- Clean periwinkles with lemon or lime juice very well to get rid of sand and grits that come with periwinkles naturally or follow clean direction on the package. Per-boil periwinkles with very little water and salt. Set aside.
- Boil stockfish. Cover with water, add some salt & boil until tender; then set aside.
- Boil assorted meat. See list & cooking direction at the end of the chapter. Then add stockfish, periwinkle and steam all for five minutes. Keep broth in.
- Chop onion, clean shredded smoked fish, clean shrimps, and set aside.

Step 2.

Extracting palm oil from fresh palm kernel (Banga):

- Clean palm kernel and boil for 30 - 40 minutes or until nuts are soft. Remove Banga

from cooking water and pour into a Mortar; pound with a pestle to separate the black seed, fiber, and the skin from the pulp.
- Add 4 cups of hot water and sieve through a colander (sifter) to drain out oil and palm kernel sauce into a deep cooking pot (discard the seed, fiber, and skin).
- Boil extracted palm oil for 10 minutes then

Step 3.

- Add meat/stockfish mixture, smoked fish, chopped onion, ground chilies and knorr or maggi cubes, Uyayak into the palm kernel oil and cook for 15 minutes. Stir occasionally.
- **If using Trafia**
- Pour it into a deep cooking pot and thaw, then pour meat/stockfish mixture, smoked fish, onion, ground chilies, knorr or maggi cubes, Uyayak and cook for 15 minutes. Stir occasionally.
- Reduce heat to medium and cook for ten (10) minutes or until the soup is fairly reduced and thickened to coat the back of the spoon.
- Add crayfish, shrimps and cook for ten (10) minutes at medium heat; then add Atama leaves and bring to boil for ten (10) minutes. Stir and add salt as needed to taste then simmer for five (5) minutes.

Serve soup over Rice or serve with pounded yam or Fufu.

Afang/Okazi/Ukazi Soup

Afang Soup is a traditional Nigerian stew from Southern part of the country (Akwa Ibom, Igbos, and Cross River State). There are different variations of this soup; especially the type of meat and fish selection.

Serves 4 or more

2 pounds Afang leaves - cleaned & chopped

1 pound Waterleaf (cleaned and chopped) or 16 oz. bag chopped frozen Spinach

1 lb. assorted meat – diced (See list & cooking direction at the end of the chapter)

1 small stockfish - cut or chopped

1 cup periwinkles - cleaned

1 cup dried prawn - chopped

2 pieces dried fish – shredded

2 tablespoon ground crayfish

1 onion - chopped

2 hot chili Pepper - hot adjust to taste

1 cup palm oil

4 Knorr or Maggi cubes

Water

Salt to taste

PREPARATION

Step 1.

- Boil stockfish. Cover with water, add some salt & boil until tender; then set aside.
- Rinse and drain Afang leaves to get rid of sediment; chopped and set aside.
- Soak Chopped Spinach in salted water for about 20 minutes; drain and set aside.
- Shred dried fish into small pieces and clean in hot water. Set aside.
- Clean periwinkles with lemon or lime juice very well to get rid of sand and grits that come with periwinkles naturally or follow clean direction on the package. Per-boil periwinkles with very little water and salt; add dried fish, stir and set aside.

Step 2.

- Boil assorted meat. See list & cooking direction at the end of the chapter. Then, add boiled stockfish and simmer for five (5) minutes. Keep stock in.
- Add periwinkles mixture, ground crayfish, waterleaves or chopped Spinach, pepper, onion and knorr or maggi, water if needed (depend on how much stock is in the meat/ stockfish mixture) then cook all for ten (10) minutes at medium heat; stir thoroughly and occasionally to prevent burning.
- Add chopped Afang leaves; crushed dried prawns, palm oil; cover and cook for fifteen (15) minutes at medium heat or until greens are soft and tender. Also to bring all the flavors together. If soup appears dry or thick add very little water at a time; add salt if needed to taste.

Serve soup with Iyan (Pounded yam), Fufu, and Eba.

Ingredients can be purchased from your local African grocery store.

1. **Afang/Ukazi/Okazi leaves** are all the same. Afang leaves are an ingredient in the popular Igbo dish. As mentioned above, the Calabar, Efik and Ibibios call it Afang, while Igbos call it Ukazi/Okazi.
2. **Periwinkles** are form of snails. They are much smaller than typical snails and can be described as tiny snails. As with regular snails, they need to be thoroughly cleaned to get rid of grit and dirt from their natural habitat. You can purchase them at your local African grocery store. They can be purchased already out of shell but still need to be clean very well or the soup would be totally ruined with sand and grits.
3. Periwinkles are also known as **Ishan in Yoruba** with different variations in spelling.
4. **Waterleaves** are also known as "**Gbure**" in Yoruba. Substitute Spinach for waterleaves.

Banga Soup (Palm Kernel Soup)

This Soup is made from Palm Kernel Fruit.

Serves many

80 -100 bangas (fresh palm kernel) seeds

1 10oz. chopped Okra – chopped into tiny pieces

1 small stockfish – chopped

1 lb. assorted meat - cut or cubes (See list & cooking direction at the end of the chapter)

2 tablespoon ground Crayfish

2 pieces dried fish - shredded

1 tablespoon Ugu (Bitter leaf) - optional

1 medium onion

1 tablespoon ground hot red pepper (adjust to taste)

4 maggi or knorr cubes

3 - 4 cups water

Salt to taste

PREPARATION

Step 1.

- Boil stockfish. Cover with water, add some salt & boil until tender; then set aside.
- Shred dried fish into small pieces and clean with hot water. Set aside.
- Chop onion, Okra and set aside.
- Boil assorted meat. See list & cooking direction at the end of the chapter; then add stockfish. Keep stock and set aside.

Step 2.

Extracting palm oil from fresh palm kernel (Banga):
- Clean palm kernel and boil for 30 minutes or until soft and tender.
- Remove from cooking water and pour into a Mortar; pound with a pestle to separate the black seed, fiber, and the skin from the pulp. Add 4 cups of the hot water and sieve through a colander (sifter) to drain out oil and palm kernel source into a deep cooking pot (discard the seed, fiber, and skin) and boil for ten minutes.

Step 3.

- Add meat/stockfish mixture into the extracted palm oil; dried fish, chopped onion, red hot pepper and knorr or maggi; then cook for 15 minutes.
- Add Ugu (bitter leaf) and ground crayfish; stir and reduce heat to medium; cook for 15 minutes until the soup is fairly reduced and thickened to coat the back of the spoon. Occasionally stir soup to allow ingredients to mix evenly and to prevent burning the soup.
- Now add Chopped Okra and cook for another ten (10) minutes. Add very little water if soup appears thick or cook longer to thicken the soup before adding okra.
- Add salt as needed.

Serve with Iyan (pounded Yam), Eba, Semolina or Fufu.

Edikang Ikong Soup

This vegetable soup is very rich and delicious. It is commonly served as a delicacy during very special ceremonies.

Serves many

3 lbs. fresh Ugu/pumpkin leaves –washed and shredded

2 10 oz. Frozen Spinach or Waterleaf

6 Snails – cleaned

1 small stockfish - Chopped

2 lbs. assorted meat – diced (See list & cooking direction at the end of the chapter)

Some Chicken gizzard

2 pieces dry fish

4 pieces crabs - cut the body into 2 pieces each.

1lb. periwinkles – top & tail – cleaned

2 tablespoon whole dry Prawns – cleaned

2 tablespoon ground crayfish

1 medium onion

1 tablespoon hot pepper

1 - 2 cups palm oil

4 - 6 maggi or knorr cubes

2 - 4 cups of water

Salt to taste

PREPARATION

Step 1.

- Remove snails and periwinkles from shells and clean thoroughly to remove sand and grits that come with them naturally or follow clean direction on the package. Use lemon or lime juice to remove slime; set aside.
- Clean crabs thoroughly and divide into two each. Combine periwinkles, snails, and crabs and boil with salt; set aside.
- Clean dry fish; drain and add to crabs/snails mixture.

- Boil stockfish. Cover with water, add some salt & boil until tender; then add chicken gizzard and boil together.
- Boil assorted meat: See list & cooking direction at the end of the chapter.
- Combine all the meat, gizzard, periwinkles, snails, crabs, prawns, pepper, knorr or maggi and simmer for 15 minutes at medium heat. Add more water if needed and keep the broth.

Step 2.

- Add shredded Ugwu/pumpkin leaves and Spinach or Waterleaf; mix thoroughly and cook for 15 minutes; stir in-between to avoid burning the soup; then add ground crayfish and palm oil; stir and reduce heat to medium; simmer for about 15-20 minutes.
- Add salt if needed to taste.

Serve Soup with Iyan (pounded Yam), Eba, Amala, Semolina or Fufu.

Gbegiri Soup (Beans Soup)

Serves many

1lb. bag blackeye peas or African red beans

1 large dried fish (shredded)

½ tablespoon ground crayfish

½ tablespoon red hot pepper (optional)

1 medium onion - chopped

1/3 cup palm oil

3 maggi or knorr cubes - crushed

6 - 8 cups of Water

Salt to taste

PREPARATION

Cleaning the beans

- Cleaning of Blackeye Peas or African Red Beans: See end of the chapter for direction on how to clean beans.
- Shred dried fish into tiny pieces and wash in hot water to remove any sand; set aside.

Cooking

- Combine beans, onion, 6-8 cups of water or cover the beans to the top and cook in a deep cooking pot until very soft and tender.
- Mash beans until it turns into puree or soupy but not watery; then add shredded dried fish, pepper, ground crayfish, maggi or knorr; cook for ten (10) minutes. Stir soup during cooking to avoid burning.
- Add palm oil and continue cooking for ten (10) minutes. Reduce heat to low and simmer for 10 - 15 minutes; stir soup intermittently.
- Salt as needed to taste.

Serve with Tuwo, Amala or Fufu with any meat stew.

Miya Tanse Soup

1 lb. meat – cut or diced

1 lb. smoked meat – cut or diced

1 16 oz. bag Spinach

2 medium size fresh tomatoes - chopped

1 medium onion – chopped

2 pieces chili pepper - chopped

1 cup groundnut - blend

2 - 3 maggi or knorr cubes

Water

Oil

Salt to taste

PREPARATION

Step 1.

- Boil meat and smoked meat with seasoning until tender. Set aside.
- Soak spinach in salted water for 15 minutes; drain and set aside.
- In a cooking pot, add some oil, fry chopped onion, tomatoes and pepper then add boiled meat, maggi and continue cooking for ten (10) minutes. Add little water if needed.
- Add groundnut and cook for 15 minutes.
- Add smoked meat, vegetable and simmer for ten (10) minutes. Add salt if needed to taste.

Serve with Tuwo

Ofe-Owerri Soup

This is classic Oweri soup flavored with aromatic Uzouza leaves and lightly thickened with Cocoyam. There are different variations of this soup, depending on the type of meats, vegetables and fish used.

Serves many

16 oz. Okazi/Ukazi leaves – shredded and cleaned

1 cup Ugu/pumpkin leaves or 1 10oz. bag Collard greens

1 lb. cocoyam - boiled and pounded to soft paste

1 ½ lbs. assorted meat – See list & cooking direction at the end of the chapter - cut or cubes

1 small stockfish – cut or chopped

2 pieces smoked fish – shredded

6 pieces snail

1lb. periwinkles – cleaned

8oz. dry Prawns – cleaned

1 tbsp. ground hot pepper – adjust to taste

2 tbsp. ground dried crayfish

1 onion - chopped

3 - 4 maggi or knorr cubes

1 cup palm oil

Salt to taste

PREPARATION

- If using Collard greens and Chopped spinach, thaw and soak in salted water for about 20 minutes; drain and set aside.
- Wash cocoyam and peel; cook until soft; drain left over water and pound to form paste. Set aside.
- Shred dried fish into small pieces and clean in hot water. Set aside.
- Remove snails and periwinkles from shells and clean thoroughly to remove sand and grits that come with them naturally or follow clean direction on the package. Use lemon or lime juice to remove slime; per-boil and set aside.
- Cover stockfish with water and boil with some salt until tender.

- Boil assorted meat with any meat seasoning: See list & cooking direction at the end of the chapter. Then, add snails/periwinkles mixture, stockfish, smoked fish, dry Prawns, pepper, onion and knorr or maggi; simmer all for about 10 - 15 minutes.
- Now form the pounded cocoyam into small balls and add to the soup; stir thoroughly.
- Add ground crayfish, palm oil and simmer for 20 minutes.
- Now add shredded Okazi/Ukazi leaves, Ugu/pumpkin leaves; cover and cook at medium heat for 10 minutes or until greens are tender. Stir thoroughly and occasionally to prevent burning.
- Add salt to taste if needed.

Serve soup with Iyan (pounded yam), Eba or Fufu.

Oha/Ora Soup

This is a very traditional soup and similar to bitter leaf soup but make with tender Ora leaves.

Serves many

16 oz. Oha/Ora leaves – chopped leaves with hand to prevent discoloration of leaves.

6 Coco yams

1 small stockfish - chopped

1 ½ lbs. assorted beef – See list & cooking direction at the end of the chapter - cut or diced

2 pieces dried fish - shredded

1 tablespoon ground crayfish

1 tablespoon ground hot red pepper

1 tablespoon iru or ogiri – optional (local spice)

3 maggi or knorr cubes

½ - 1 cup palm oil

Salt to taste

PREPARATION

- Wash, peel and cook cocoyam until very soft; pound to a smooth paste and set aside.
- In a deep pot, cover stockfish with water and boil with some salt until tender; set aside.
- Cut or diced meat; boil with onion and little salt until tender; remove excess broth from the meat and replace with water; add stockfish and cook for five (5) minutes.
- Add crayfish, dried fish, pepper, iru/ogiri, maggi and cook for ten (10) minutes. Occasionally stir soup to prevent burning and to allow ingredients to mix evenly.
- Add cocoyam paste in small lumps; palm oil; cover and cook until all the cocoyam lumps have dissolved. Add more water if soup appears too thick little by little.
- Add Ora leaves and simmer for ten (10) minutes.
- Add salt if needed to taste.

Serve with Eba, Fufu, Semolina or Amala.

Ottong Soup

Serves many

1 ½ lbs. assorted meat - cubes (See list & cooking direction at the end of the chapter)

1 small stockfish

2 pieces smoked or dried fish

1 lb. periwinkle (remove the shell)

1 cup shrimps - optional

2 tablespoons ground crayfish

1 10oz. bag Okra - chopped

¼ cup Blended Ogbono

8oz. Ugwu/pumpkin leaves

1 tablespoon ground hot red pepper (adjust to taste)

1 medium onion - chopped

½ - 1 cup palm oil

4 maggi or knorr cubes

Water

Salt to taste

PREPARATION

Step1:

- Chop Okra; set aside. Thaw shrimps and set aside.
- Wash, shred, and soak Ugwu/pumpkin leaves for about 15 - 20 minutes in salted water; drain and set aside.
- Shred smoked dried fish into small pieces and wash in hot water. Set aside.
- Clean periwinkles thoroughly to remove sand and grits that come with it naturally or follow clean direction on the package. Use lemon or lime juice to remove slime. Set aside.
- Cover stockfish with water and boil with some salt until tender; set aside.
- Boil assorted: See list & cooking direction at the end of the chapter. Then reduce heat and add stockfish, smoked fish, periwinkle, pepper, onion, maggi or knorr cubes and

about 2-3 cups of water if needed or broth in the meat may be enough; simmer for ten (10) minutes; reduce heat to low to get Ogbono ready.

Step 2: Preparing Ogbono

Method One:
- In a small cooking pot, add half the palm oil and heat a little; reduce heat to medium; stir in Apon/Ogbono slowly and stir constantly as you add Ogbono; fry for two (2) minutes (do not over fry or burn). Reduce heat if necessary.
- Stir in two (2) cups of water (as you stir in the water, Apon/Agbono will rise up and draw). Continue stirring until a smooth consistency is obtained and lump free. Cook for ten (10) minutes at medium heat. If Ogbono appears thick, add little water.

Method Two:
- Bring one cup of water to boil; stir in Ogbono slowly and stir constantly; as you add Ogbono will rise up and draw; continue stirring until a smooth consistency is obtained and lump free; then add two (2) cups of water and cook for ten (10) minutes.
- Add Ogbono to meat/stockfish mixture and mix thoroughly; add ground crayfish, shrimps and cook for another fifteen (15) minutes. Stir occasionally during cooking to prevent burning.
- Add Ugwu/pumpkin leaves and cook for ten (10) minutes or until tender; add chopped Okra and allow to bubble for five (5) minutes; then reduce heat to low and simmer for 5 minutes. Add salt if needed to taste.

Serve soup with Eba, Amala, Iyan, Semolina or Fufu.

Seafood Soup

Serves many

1 pound shrimp
4 - 5 pieces crabs – cut into 2 each
1 large onion – chopped
2 clove garlic – chopped
1 large green bell pepper – chopped
2 28-oz. can tomato
1 16-oz. can tomato sauce
1 bay leaf
1 teaspoon basil
½ teaspoon oregano leaves
¼ cup olive oil

PREPARATION

- Clean and boil crabs; set aside.
- In a frying pan or saucepan, sauté onion, garlic and green bell pepper in olive oil.
- Add tomato, tomato sauce, bay leaf, basil and oregano; stir well and bring to boil; reduce heat and simmer for 20 minutes.
- Add crab and shrimp; cover and simmer ten (10) minutes; remove bay leaf and discard
- Serve hot over rice.

Note: This soup can also be prepared with fresh fish, for example fresh Tilapia.

Ukpo Soup

This very rich Okra and vegetable soup is from the South East region of Nigeria. Therefore, there are different variations; especially the type of meats, fish or sea food selections.

Serves many

4 Ukpo Seeds
1 small stockfish - chopped
1 lb. Fish (Mackerel or Catfish) – cut into pieces
1 lb. beef - diced
8oz. Okazi
4oz. dried fish
1 tablespoon ground crayfish
2 tablespoon dadawa or Iru
½ - 1 tbsp. ground hot red pepper – adjust to taste
3-4 maggi or knorr cubes
½ cup palm oil
Salt to taste

PREPARATION

Step 1.

- Serve with Eba, Iyan, Fufu, or Semolina
- Crack Ukpo seeds and boil for 1½ - 2 hours or until soft and tender.
- Pour hot Ukpo into a Mortar and Pound with a pestle; add some palm oil and pound until it is powdery. Set aside.
- Soak Okazi in hot water and set aside.
- In a deep pot, cover stockfish with water and boil with some salt until tender; set aside.
- Cut or diced meat; boil with onion and two (2) maggi or knorr cubes until tender; then add fish and boil together for about 10 minutes; remove fish and set aside. Then add stockfish to meat and boil for view minutes.
- Add crayfish, dried fish, dadawa (Iru), palm oil, remaining maggi if needed and pepper; cook for another ten (10) minutes. Occasionally stir soup to prevent burning and to allow ingredients to mix evenly. If needed add about ½ to one cup of water; stir and cook for five (5) minutes.
- Add Ukpo, fish, stir and cook 10 minutes covered; add Okazi and cook for another 5 - 10 minutes.
- Add salt if needed to taste.

White Soup/NSala

Serves many

1 Big Fresh Cat Fish – clean and cut into small sizes
3 pieces sliced Yam or ½ cup Yam Flour – as thickener
1 tablespoon Crayfish
1 tablespoon Ogiri
2 habanera pepper – Blend (optional)
1 medium onion
1 tablespoon cleaned Utazi or bitter leaf
3 maggi or knorr cubes
8 -10 cups of water
Salt to taste

PREPARATION

Step 1.

- Clean and cut cat fish into small to medium size; add boiled water, this will harden the pieces and will not dissolve while cooking.
- Dice pieces of sliced yam and boil yam until soft; pound to form a smooth paste or mix yam flour with cold water to get smooth thick paste. Set aside
- Combine eight (8) cups of water, blended habanera, Utazi or bitter leaf, chopped onion, maggi or knorr cubes and cook for ten (10) minutes.
- Add cat fish, crayfish and ogiri; cover and cook for 15 minutes at medium high; stir intermittently to allow ingredients to mix evenly and to avoid burning.
- Add yam paste in small lumps; cover and allow the soup to cook and bubble, the yam past should dissolve.
- If the soup appears too thick, add water a little at a time or add more yam paste for a thicker soup. Add salt to taste. Enjoy!

Serve with Eba, Amala, Fufu or Semolina.

Assorted Meats

Goat meat, beef, chicken, smoked turkey, oxtail, beef tripe, cow skin (pomo), cow legs (bokoto), snail, and stockfish.

How to Cook Assorted Meat

- In a deep cooking pot, boil assorted meat with any meat seasoning until tender. Meat and honeycomb (tripe) will become tender before pomo (cow skin); so, remove these and continue cooking pomo until tender or boil pomo (cow skin) separately.

- Add meat and honeycomb back to pomo after it is done and cook together for view minutes.

- Remove any leftover meat stock from the meat and filter to remove any sediment and floating fat before pouring it back in the meat.

How to cook stockfish

- In a deep pot, cover stockfish with water, pinch of salt and boil until tender.

Cleaning of Blackeye Peas or African Red Beans

- Soak blackeye peas in cold water for about five minutes. This will allow the beans to swell and make it easier to remove the outer coat or pour a small amount of the beans into the blender, cover with water; grind for about 3 – 5 seconds (do not blend) and pour the beans into a large bowl; continue the process until finish.
- Cover beans with water; rub beans in between palms of both hands back and forth in the water to loosing the outer coat. The outer coat will naturally float to the top.
- Use a strainer to separate beans from the outer coat by draining the floating coats. Continue this process until beans is cleaned and no more coats or dark sport. Filter and change water as many times as needed.

CHAPTER 4

Lunch or Dinner Dishes: Pepper Soups

Spicy Mixed Goat Meat Pepper Soup with Bitter Leaf

Serves many

3 lb. assorted meat (See list at the end of the chapter) - diced

2 tablespoon pepper soup seasoning

2 habanera – chopped (hot adjust to taste)

1 large onion

2 tablespoon crayfish

1 tablespoon bitter leaf

3 maggi or knorr cubes

8 -10 cups of water

PREPARATION

- Boil assorted meat: see end of Chapter 3 for list and how.
- Add six (6) cups of water, pepper soup seasoning, crayfish, bitter leaf, habanera and simmer for 20 - 25 minutes. Occasionally stir soup to allow ingredients to mix evenly.
- Add more water in needed and salt to taste.

Pepper Soup seasonings are mixture of local herbs and spices and are not readily available in most supermarkets except in stores specializing in African Foods.

Catfish Pepper Soup

Serves many

1 Big Fresh Catfish – cut into small to medium sizes

1 tablespoon pepper soup seasoning

2 habanera – chopped (hot adjust to taste)

1 large onion - chopped

1 tablespoon ground crayfish

1 tablespoon chopped parsley leave

3 maggi or knorr cubes

8 -10 cups of water

PREPARATION

- Cut and clean catfish, then pour boiled water over it before cooking. This will harding the pieces and keep the pieces from breaking up during cooking.
- Combine eight (8) cups of water, pepper soup seasoning, habanera, chopped onion, maggi or knorr cubes and cook for 10 minutes.
- Add catfish, cover and cook for 15 minutes at medium high; add parsley lower heat to low and simmer for 5 - 10 minutes. Occasionally stir to allow ingredients to mix evenly.
- Add salt to taste and serve hot.

Isi-Ewu (Goat Head Pepper Soup)

Serves many

1 Goat head and legs – clean & cut into small pieces

3 habanera peppers – hot, adjust to taste

4 fresh tomatoes

1 large onion

4 tablespoon tomato paste

2 clove garlic

Ginger – to taste

3 teaspoon Lemon juice

1 tbsp. pepper soup seasoning

1 tbsp. Ugu - Bitter leaf - optional

4 maggi or knorr cubes

½ cup palm oil

8 - 10 cups water

Salt to taste

PREPARATION

- Blend fresh tomato, habanera peppers, onion, garlic, ginger and tomato paste. Set aside.
- Clean goat head and the legs very well to remove any grits and hair then cut into small pieces; remove any parts that you do not want; add lemon juice, mix and marinate for about 20 minutes.
- In a large deep cooking pot, add goat, eight (8) cups of water, two (2) maggi or knorr cubes and cook until soft and tender; add more water if needed. Reduce heat to medium heat.
- Add tomato/pepper mixture, ugu (better leaf), pepper soup seasoning, remaining maggi cover and cook for 20 minutes. Stir occasionally to prevent burning; add palm oil and simmer for another 15 minutes at low heat.
- Add salt to taste and water if needed to thin out soup and serve hot.

CHAPTER 5

Lunch or Dinner Dishes: Rice

Baked Rice

Serves 10 or more

5 cups uncooked rice
8 cups of water
1 small onion – finely chopped
¼ cup celery – finely chopped
¼ cup finely chopped green and red bell peppers
¼ cup olive oil or butter
½ teaspoon garlic powder
Salt to taste

DIRECTION:

- In a deep cooking pot add oil or butter; add rice and stir fry until golden brown (stir constantly to avoid burning); add eight (8) cups of water to per-boil rice for about ten (10) minutes.
- Turn the heat off; add chopped onion, celery, bell peppers and garlic powder; stir and add salt to taste.
- Pour rice into a 9 X 13-inch baking dish; cover with foil; bake at 350 degrees for fifty (50) minutes or until rice is cooked.
- Add more water for softer rice.

Serve with baked chicken, fish or steak.

Coconut Rice

Serves 8 or more

4 cups of Rice
6 cups coconut milk
1 lb. boneless chicken - diced
1 lb. shrimp
1 tablespoon ground crayfish or to taste
1 large red bell peppers – diced
1 large fresh tomatoes – diced
½ tablespoon ground pepper or to taste
1 large carrots - diced
1 medium onion - chopped
1/4 cup oil
4 maggi or knorr cubes
Water
Salt to taste

PREPARATION

Step 1.

- Boil chicken with onion and some maggi until tender, cool then dice. Thaw shrimp, drain and set aside.
- Using fresh coconut fruit: crack 3 coconuts open; remove the white flesh and roughly grate;
- Pour hot water to cover grated coconut and leave to stand for about 30 minutes.
- Remove the roughage by press and squeeze the flesh to extract the milk; then sieve the liquid to remove any leftover roughage. The more water, the thinner the milk will be. In general, one fresh coconut will yield about 2 cups of milk **or** use two cans of coconut milk.
- Boil coconut milk for about ten (10) minutes at medium heat; add rice and cook until almost done.
- Add chicken, tomatoes, pepper, maggi or knorr and oil; stir and reduce heat to low, cover and simmer until rice is done and the liquid is absorbed. However, if water is needed add little by little. Do not add too much water or the rice will be mushy or soggy.
- Add diced carrots, red bell pepper, ground crayfish, stir and steam for 5-10 minutes then add shrimp, salt to taste if needed; steam for view minutes.

Serve with Dodo, Moin-Moin and any vegetable.
For Meat: Baked Chicken, Fried Chicken, Baked Fish, Fried Fish or Steak.

Fried Rice

There are many variations of fried rice, each with its own specific ingredients.

Serves 10 or more

5 cups Rice

1 lb. Shrimp

1 cup cooked chicken gizzards – diced into tiny pieces

1 10oz. pkg. frozen peas & carrots

1 large onion - diced

Garlic - to taste (chopped)

4 maggi or knorr cubes - crushed

Thyme to taste

1 cup oil or butter

Water

Salt to taste

PREPARATION

- Clean and boil gizzards with some salt until tender; cool then dice and set aside
- Drain water out of shrimp and peas/carrot vegetable. Set them aside.
- Add oil or butter into a deep cooking pot and heat over medium heat; add garlic and stir fry for one minute; add rice; stir fry (stir continuously to avoid burning) for about 10 minutes or until rice is brown (not burn).
- Add seven (7) cups of water, maggi or knorr cubes, thyme, sliced onion, mix thoroughly, (add about ½ to one cup of water if needed); cover and steam for 20 to 30 minutes or until water is absorb completely into the rice. Do not add too much water or the rice will be mushy or soggy.
- Open and stir rice; add boiled gizzard; vegetable, stir and steam for another 10 minutes or until rice is cooked; add shrimp and steam for 5 minutes.
- Add salt to taste if needed.

Serve with: Dodo, Moin-Moin, Beans, and vegetable.

Meat: Baked Chicken, Fried Chicken, Baked Fish, Fried Fish or Steak.

Jollof Rice

Serves 10 or more

5 cups Rice
1 15oz. can tomato sauce
2 large fresh tomatoes
1 6oz. can tomato paste
1 medium onion
2 habanera peppers (hot, adjust to taste)
2 red bell peppers
Garlic to taste
4 maggi or knorr cubes
Curry powder to taste
Ground thyme to taste
5 pieces bay leaves
½ -1 cup of oil
Water
Salt to taste

PREPARATION

- Blend tomato sauce, fresh tomatoes, paste, onion, garlic, habanera peppers, and red bell peppers together. Add very little water as needed during blending for the blade to rotate.
- Pour blended tomato/pepper mixture into a deep cooking pot; add maggi or knorr cubes, thyme, curry; six (6) cups of water, stir and cook for 15 minutes at medium heat.
- Reduce heat to low heat; wash rice and rinse to remove excess starch; add rice to tomato/pepper mixture; stir thoroughly; add oil, bay leaves; mix and cover; steam until all the liquid is absorbed into the rice; then open and stir thoroughly. Add water if needed for softer rice; but too much water, the rice will be mushy or soggy.
- Add salt if needed and simmer for 5 - 10 minutes.

Serve with: Dodo, Moin-Moin, any green vegetables.

Meat: Baked Chicken, Fried Chicken, Baked Fish, Fried Fish or Steak.

Rice and Beans Porridge

Serves 8 or more

2 cups Rice
1 lb. bag blackeye peas or African Red Beans
1 15oz. can of tomato sauce
3 tbsp. tomato paste
1 medium onion
2 habanera peppers (hot, adjust to taste)
1 red bell pepper
Garlic to taste
3 - 4 maggi or knorr cubes
½ -1 cup palm oil or 1/3 cup oil
Water
Salt to taste

PREPARATION

- Blend tomato sauce, paste, onion, garlic, habanera peppers, and red bell pepper together. Add very little water as needed during blending for the blade to rotate. Set aside.
- Soak blackeye peas in cold water for about five minutes. (This will allow the beans to swell up and make it easy to remove the outer coat); or pour small amount of the beans into the blender, cover with water; grind for about 3 – 5 seconds (do not blend) and pour the beans into a large bowl; continue the process until finish.
- Cover beans with water; rub beans in between palms of both hands back and forth in the water to loosen the outer coat. The outer coat will naturally float to the top.
- Use a strainer to separate beans from the outer coat by draining the floating coats. Continue this process until beans is cleaned and no more coats or dark sport. Filter and change water as many times as needed.
- Pour cleaned bean into a deep cooking pot; cover with water and cook on medium high heat for 20 minutes to cook the bean half way done.
- Wash rice and rinse to remove excess starch; add to cooking beans; mix; cover and cook together for 15 – 20 minutes. Reduce heat if needed to prevent burning. Also you may need to add more water to the beans and rice if all the liquid is absorbed into the porridge while rice or beans is not done.
- Add tomato/pepper mixture, maggi or knorr cubes, thyme, curry, palm oil; stir, cover and steam for 15 minutes or until porridge is cooked at low heat to avoid burning. Also Stir porridge intermittently and continue simmering until done.
- Add salt if needed.

Rice and Chicken Casserole

Serves 4 or more

1 cup uncooked rice
2 lbs. boneless chicken breast – remove skin and dice
1 10¾ oz. can condensed cream of mushroom
1 10¾ oz. can condensed cream of broccoli or celery
1 medium onion – dice
2 tablespoon olive oil or butter
2 14½ oz. can French style green beans rinse and drain
1 large red bell paper
1½ - 2 cup grated cheddar cheese
Salt to taste

PREPARATION

Preheat oven to 350 degrees F.

- Clean and dice the chicken; per boil with some maggi for about five (5) minutes. Do not add water. Wash rice and rinse to remove excess starch.
- Heat oil or butter in a frying pan over medium heat; add onion, pinch of salt, and sauté for five (5) minutes.
- Remove from heat and transfer to a large bowl; add all the remaining ingredients except cheese; stir all together thoroughly.
- Pour into a greased large casserole baking dish or pan; baked for 25-30 minutes or until bubbly;
- Add cheese and bake for 10 minutes.

Rice and Goat Meat and Chicken Curry

Serves 6 or more

1 lb. boneless goat meat - diced

1 lb. boneless chicken - diced

1 can 15 oz. diced tomatoes - on drained

1 medium onion - chopped

1 medium red bell pepper – chopped

1 medium green bell pepper – chopped

2 tablespoon curry powder – adjust to your taste

1 habanera pepper (optional)

1 cup chopped carrot

2 maggi cubes

Salt to taste

Water

6 - 8 cups of Cooked Rise

PREPARATION

- Clean and boil goat meat and chicken with maggi cubes; add little water as most meat produces water as it cooks; drain excess broth.
- Combine meat/chicken, tomatoes, chopped onion, red and green bell peppers, carrot, habanera, curry powder one cup of water (add more if needed); stir and bring to a boil; reduce heat to low; cover and simmer for 45 minutes. Stir periodically.
- Add salt to taste and serve over hot cook rice.

Rice and Lemon Chicken

Serves 2 - 4

6 - 8 cups of Cooked Rise

6 chicken breast halves and/or drumsticks

8 pieces potatoes

1 red bell pepper - diced

1 red onion - chopped

3 4oz. can sliced mushrooms

2 lemons – divided

¼ cup olive oil

4 large garlic cloves – chopped

2-3 teaspoon dried oregano leaves

½ teaspoons coarsely ground black pepper

Salt to taste

PREPARATION

- Using lemon zester, zest one lemon to measure 1½ tablespoons.
- Juice lemon to measure one tablespoon juice.
- In a mixing bowl, combine lemon zest, juice, oil, garlic, oregano, salt and black pepper; and mix well.
- Arrange chicken in a baking pan; brush chicken with a portion of the lemon juice mixture.
- Scrub potatoes well and pat dry and cut them in half; slice remaining lemon.
- In a mixing bowl, combine potatoes, bell pepper, onion, lemon slices and mushrooms with remaining lemon juice mixture; toss to mix.
- Arrange vegetables around chicken in the baking pan.
- Preheat oven to 400 degrees and bake chicken
- Bake for 30 minutes, then open and brush chicken and vegetables with the juice in the pan; continue baking for another 30 minutes or until chicken is done.
- Serve over rice.

Rice and Mushroom

Serves 6

5-6 cups Cooked Rice

2 8oz can slice mushroom

1 large onion – chopped

2 tablespoon olive oil

¼ lb. butter

3 tablespoon flour

2 cups milk

Salt and pepper

3 tablespoon chopped fresh parsley

½ cup dry bread crumbs

¼ cup grated Parmesan cheese

PREPARATION

- In a large frying pan, sauté onion and mushrooms with three (3) tablespoons of butter for about 10 minutes; then add three (3) tablespoons butter and stir until melted.
- Stir in flour until smooth and lump free; gradually stir in milk; add some salt, ½ teaspoon pepper.
- Bring to a boil and cook for three (3) minute; add rice and two (2) tablespoon parsley; mix and pour mixture into a 2-qt casserole pan; top with cheese and bake at 350 degrees.
- Serve with baked chicken, fish or steak.

CHAPTER 6

Lunch or Dinner Dishes: Others

Asaro (Yam Porridge)

Serves 5 or more

1 Large AfricanYam

1 15oz. can tomato sauce

3 tablespoon tomato paste

1 medium onion

2 habaneras or chili peppers (hot, adjust to taste)

1 red bell pepper

Garlic to taste

1tablespoon ground crayfish

2 maggi or knorr cubes

3 - 4 tablespoon brown or white sugar - adjust to taste

½ cup palm oil or 1/3 oil

Water

½ teaspoon salt

PREPARATION

- Blend tomato sauce, tomato paste, onion, garlic, habanera peppers, and red bell peppers. Add enough water for the blade to rotate during blending; set aside.
- Peel yam; slice into small pieces; wash in cold water and pour into a deep cooking pot.
- Add 3 cups of water, salt, and sugar; cover and cook yam until almost cook and reduce heat to low heat.
- Add tomato/pepper mixture, maggi or knorr cubes, palm oil and mix thoroughly; (add little water if needed for loose porridge); cover and cook until yam is soft at low heat. Stir occasionally during cooking to avoid burning.
- Mash some of the pieces of the yam, add crayfish and stir thoroughly; then steam for 5 - 10 minutes at low heat.

Serve with dodo (fried Plantain) and fish or meat fried stew.

Substitute Potatoes for Yam.

Ewa Adalu (Beans and Sweet Corn Porridge)

Serves many

1 lb. bag blackeye peas or African Red Beans

1 15¼ oz. can sweet corn or 2 cups fresh corn

1 tablespoon ground crayfish

1 15oz. can tomato sauce

1 tablespoon tomato paste

1 small onion

Garlic - to taste

Fresh ginger - to taste

1-2 habaneras pepper

2 maggi or knorr cubes

Brown sugar to taste

1/3 cup palm oil

Water

Salt to taste

PREPARATION

- Blend tomato sauce, paste, onion, ginger, garlic and habanera peppers together. Add very little water during blending; but enough for blade to rotate. Set aside.
- Cover beans with water and bring to boil; drain and repeat this process twice. This will clean beans and reduce foaming.
- Add sugar and 4 - 5 cups of water and cook beans until soft and tender. Add more water if needed to cook the beans.
- Reduce heat to low heat, add mixture of pepper/tomato, ground crayfish, maggi cubes and mix thoroughly; cook 15 minutes; occasionally stir to prevent burning.
- Add sweet corn, palm oil and simmer for 10-15 minutes at low heat
- Add salt to taste and water if needed; simmer for 5 minutes.
- Serve with Dodo or Chips.

Ekuru ati Ata Din-din (Steamed Savory Beans and Pepper Stew)

Serves many

1 lb. bag blackeye peas or African Red Beans

1 tablespoon ground crayfish

3 pieces dry fish – clean & shredded

1 15oz. can tomato sauce

1 tablespoon tomato paste

1 small onion

1 red bell pepper

Garlic - to taste

Fresh ginger - to taste

1- 2 habaneras pepper

2 - 3 maggi or knorr cubes

½ cup palm oil or oil adjust to taste

Salt to taste

PREPARATION

Step 1:

- Cleaning of Blackeye Peas or African Red Beans: See end of the chapter.

Blend Cleaned Beans

- Blend the beans into smooth paste; add water as needed for the blender to rotate. However, do not add too much or it will become watery. Beans batter (paste) should be a little thinner than cake batter.

Step 2:

- Make pouches/pockets with aluminum foil or use individual non-stick cup-cake cups.
- Pour blended beans into a mixing bowl and mix well until it is well aerated and light. Use warm water if needed gradually).

- Scoop beans mixture into the aluminum pouches one by one; fill it half-way to allow room for expansion during cooking. Seal the foil at the top by folding several times.
- Arrange into a deep cooking pot and add about 4 cups of water. Add more water as needed. Cook for 30 - 45 minutes; Open one, it should be firm to the touch when cooked.

Step 3:

Make Fried Pepper Stew
- Blend tomato sauce, paste, onion, ginger, garlic, habanera peppers, and red bell pepper together; add very little water during blending but enough for the blade to rotate.
- Pour palm oil into deep cooking pot and heat at medium heat; add pepper/tomato mixture, maggi or knorr, cover and cook for 30 minutes at low heat or until fairly reduced to thick paste; stir occasionally during cooking to prevent burning.
- Add ground crayfish, shredded dry fish and continue cooking a low heat. Oil should float to the top. Add salt if needed to taste.

Step 4:

- Open some of the cooked Ekuru into a bowl and mash; then add fried pepper stew and stir thoroughly then serve with Eko.

Serve with Éko (Corn Powder Jelly) or eat alone.

Ikokore (Water-Yam Porridge)

Serves many

1 large African Water-Yam

2 pieces dried fish – shredded

1 Tablespoon ground crayfish

1 15oz. can tomato sauce or 3 large fresh tomatoes

3 tablespoon tomato paste

1 medium onion

1-2 habaneras or chili peppers

1 red bell pepper

3 maggi or knorr cubes

½ cup palm oil or oil – adjust to taste

Water

Salt to taste

PREPARATION

- Blend tomato sauce or fresh tomatoes, tomato paste, onion, habanera peppers, and red bell peppers. Add enough water for the blade to rotate during blending; set aside.
- Peel water-yam; wash in cold water; grate into a clean bowl and season with a dash of salt; roll grated yam into small balls and set aside.
- Pour blended tomato/pepper mixture into a cooking pot; add crayfish, maggi or knorr cubes, 2 - 3 cups of water and cook for 10 minutes. Add dried fish, palm oil, stir and cook for 20 minutes at medium heat.
- Reduce heat to low heat and drop each water-yam ball into the simmering soup to form dumplings.
- Cover the pot and steam for 30 minutes or until yam is cooked. Open and stir Porridge thoroughly to mix all the ingredients together. Add water little by little for loose Ikokore.
- Add salt if needed to taste; stir and steam for another five (5) minutes.

Serve hot.

Nigerian Cabbage Salad

This is a mixture of fresh vegetables and fruits and cold and hot.

Serves many

2 cans baked beans

1- 2 cans mackerel or sardine fish

3 - 4 eggs – Boil and Sliced

1 cabbage – shredded

3 pieces carrot - shredded

2 cucumbers - diced

3 Fresh tomatoes - diced

1 large green pepper - diced

1 large red pepper - diced

1 small red or yellow sweet onion - sliced

Mayonnaise - to taste

PREPARATION

- Add boil water to shredded cabbage in a bowl and soak for five (5) minutes; drain and dry to remove excess water from the cabbage.
- In a mixing bowl, combine cabbage, carrot, cucumber, green and red pepper, onion and toss; add baked beans and mix; then add mayonnaise (to taste) and mix thoroughly.
- Add fish and mix thoroughly; garnish with sliced eggs and diced tomatoes.
- Keep in the fridge until ready to serve.

How to Clean Blackeye Peas or African Red Beans

- Soak blackeye peas in cold water for about five minutes. (This will allow the beans to swell up and make it easy to remove the outer coat); or pour small amount of the beans into the blender, cover with water; grind for about 3 – 5 seconds (do not blend) and pour the beans into a large bowl; continue the process until finish.
- Cover beans with water; rub beans in between palms of both hands back and forth in the water to loosen the outer coat. The outer coat will naturally float to the top.
- Use a strainer to separate beans from the outer coat by draining the floating coats. Continue this process until beans is cleaned and no more coats or dark sport. Filter and change water as many times as needed.

CHAPTER 7

Snacks

Akara (Beans Patties)

Serves many

1 lb. Bag Blackeye Peas or African Red Beans
1 small red bell pepper
1 small to medium onion
2 maggi or knorr cubes – crushed
2 cups water
Oil or African palm oil – to fry
Salt to taste

PREPARATION

- Cleaning of Blackeye Peas or African Red Beans: See end of Chapter 1or 6.

Blending

- Combine cleaned beans, bell pepper, onion and blend. Add water as needed for the blender to rotate; however, do not add too much water or beans will become watery. Beans batter (paste) should be as thick as Pancake batter.
- Pour blended beans into a mixing bowl; add crushed maggi cubes and salt if needed. Mix thoroughly until lump free and light.

Frying:

- Deep-fry the mixture by scooping a little amount individually into hot oil and fry until golden. Scoop as many as the frying pan will take.
- Continue the process until finished.
- Serve hot or cool.

Boli ati Epa (Roasted Plantain and Peanuts)

Serves 1-2

2 semi-ripe Plantains

Peanuts

PREPARATION

- Roast plantains in the oven or on the grill and serve hot.
- Serve with peanuts, butter or margarine.

Buns (Nigerian Donuts)

Serves 25 and up

½ bag 5 lbs. All-purpose flour

1 ½ - 2 cups of sugar or adjust to taste

6 large eggs

1 cup butter

1 teaspoon salt

9 - 10 tablespoon water

PREPARATION:

- In a large mixing bowl add flour and knead in butter; add sugar and salt.
- Add eggs and knead; add water little by little and knead into dropping consistency.

Frying:

- Pour oil into a deep fryer and heat. Test the oil by dropping a little batter into the hot oil; batter should float to the top.
- Roll batter into individual balls (determine the size) and gently drop into the hot oil or batter can be scooped up by forming a scoop with your hand and scoop up the batter and gently drop into the hot oil. Please be careful with this method.
- Deep fry until light brown or golden brown. Make sure buns are fried through to the inner part. Remove and drain excess oil.
- Serve hot. Okay to warm in the microwave oven.

Chin-Chin

Makes about 2 gallons

5 cups All-purpose flour

2 cups unsalted butter or margarine – cubed and keep cold

4 Egg yokes

8 tablespoons cold water

1 - 1½ cups Sugar or to taste

PREPARATION

Step 1.

- Combine flour and butter in a mixing bowl and knead; then add egg yolks, sugar, and knead the dough.
- Add the cold water gradually little by little into the dough and knead to form soft but firm dough.
- Roll dough into a ball and wrap with clear plastic wrap and let it rest for about three (3) hours in the fridge.

Step 2.

- Then divide dough into 8 or 10 balls.
- Sprinkle some flour on a cutting board or other flat surface.
- Place one dough ball on the cutting board and flatten until it is about ½ inch thick.
- Cut into ropes then cut into little squares, each square about ½ inch by ½ inch thick or preference. Continue the process.

Step 3.

- Use a deep fryer or deep cooking pot; on a medium heat place some oil on the stove and allow it to heat up.
- Once oil is hot, place a few handfuls of the cut dough into the oil. The oil may foam up, this is okay; stir with a utensil gently and the oil will come down.
- Allow the chin-chin to deep fry until light or golden brown. Stir the chin-chin while frying to prevent burning.
- Place some paper napkins on a flat tray, scoop fried chin-chin on it to soak up extra oil and cool down on a flat tray.
- Store in a dry airtight container.
- Serve anytime.

Dodo (Fried Plantain)

Serves 4 to 6

6 pieces of ripped plantain

Salt to taste

Palm oil or Oil (any type)

PREPARATION:

- Slice or dice the plantain into pieces; add salt to taste.
- Pour palm oil or oil into a deep fryer or frying pan over medium high heat until hot.
- Place some cut plantain into the hot oil and fry until golden brown.
- Remove from the oil or palm oil and continue the process until finish.
- Serve hot.

Grilled or Roasted Corn

This nibble food is a street food sold on the street in Nigeria as snack.

Serve 6 or more

12 ears corn – remove from silk & husks

1 fresh coconut – crack open & remove flesh

Some salt to taste

PREPARATION

- Crack opens the coconut, removes the flesh and diced.
- Roast the coconut a little on the grill.
- Roast the corns on the grill. Turn the corns with tongs every few minutes so that it does not burn. Roast to taste.
- Serve roasted corn with roasted coconut hot or cold.

Hominy with Coconut

This is dried corn that is soaked and cooked until soft

Serve 4 or more

2 cans of Hominy corn

1 fresh coconut – crack open & remove flesh

Some salt to taste

PREPARATION

- Crack opens the coconut, removes the flesh and diced.
- Roast the coconut a little.
- Combine hominy and coconut; add some salt to taste, then steam for 5 minutes; stir thoroughly.
- Serve hot or at room temperature.

Ipekere - Plantain Chips

Serves about 4-6

6 green unripe Plantains – sliced very thin

Salt to taste

Palm oil or Oil (any type)

PREPARATION

- Peel and slice the green plantains as thin as possible.
- Sprinkle with salt to taste.
- Use a deep fryer or deep cooking pot; on a medium heat, heat some oil.
- Once the oil is hot, place some sliced plantains into the oil and fry until light or golden brown.
- Remove plantains and place on paper towels to absorb the excess oil and cool.
- Serve hot or cold anytime.

Isu Din-din/Dun-dun (Fried Yam)

Serves many

1 Large African Yam

Hot red ground pepper – optional

Salt to taste

Palm oil or Canola Oil

PREPARATION:

- Peel the skin off the yam; slice and wash in cold water.
- Drain and dry sliced yam with paper towel or air dry.
- Sprinkle with salt and pepper to taste.
- Deep fry in any oil or palm oil until golden brown.
- Drain on absorbent paper towel in the strainer.
- Serve with Beans Porridge.

Kokoro – Corn Four Chips

Serves many

2 ½ cups Corn Flour

1 cup Gari

1 cup of sugar or to taste

Oil

Salt

Water

PREPARATION

- Boil about four (4) cups of water.
- Add some water to the corn flour and mix as you add water. You want firm dough, so don't add too much water.
- Allow to cool slightly.
- Add gari and sugar; mix thoroughly with your hand to get a firm and smooth mixture (dough).
- Cut dough into several balls.
- Sprinkle some flour on a cutting board or other flat surface; roll out each dough ball to about 3 inches long; then join both ends to form a ring.
- Use a deep fryer or deep cooking pot; on a medium heat, heat oil.
- Once the oil is hot, place some Kokoro into the oil. The oil may foam up this is okay; stir with a utensil gently and the oil will come down.
- Allow the Kokoro to deep fry; continuously stir the Kokoro gently to prevent burning.
- Remove Kokoro and place on paper towels to absorb the excess oil and cool.
- Serve cool.

Meat Pie

Make 25 pies or more (depends on the size)

Meat Mixture:

1 ib. ground beef or turkey

1 ib. ground turkey sausage

2 medium peel potatoes – diced

1 10¾ oz. can Cream of Mushroom Condensed Soup

1 medium onion – chopped

1 medium red bell pepper – chopped

1 medium green bell pepper – chopped

2 pieces of habaneras or hot chili pepper – chopped

Garlic - to taste – chopped

Curry Powder to taste

½ cup Milk

2 - 3 knorr or maggi cubes

Salt to taste

When making meat pies, it is best to start with the pastry dough first. The Dough needs to rest for about 3-4 hours before use; unless refrigerated pie crusts are used.

PREPARATION: MEAT MIXTURE

- Sauté diced potatoes for about 5 minutes; then add chopped onion, bell peppers, habaneras or hot chili pepper, garlic, ginger, curry powder and maggi or knorr cubes. Add ¼ cup of water if needed and sauté; set aside.
- Brown ground beef and turkey sausage in a skillet; stirring to crumble the meat (drain any excess fat). Add pepper mixture and mix thoroughly. Set aside to cool. This gives the meat mixture to soak up any juice.

DOUGH MIXTURE:

5 cups All-purpose flour

2 ½ cups unsalted butter or margarine – cubed and keep cold

4 egg yolks

8 tablespoon cold water

3 tablespoon sugar - optional

Egg white for brushing

DIRECTIONS:

- Combine flour and butter in a mixing bowl and knead; then add egg yolks, sugar, and knead the dough.
- Then, add the cold water gradually little by little into the dough to form soft but firm dough.
- Roll dough into a ball and wrap with a clear plastic wrap; let it rest for about four (4) hours in the fridge.
- The number of pies from the dough will depend on the size of the pies.
- Roll out some dough, about 1/4 inch in thickness. Don't make it too thick.
- Take a round object, place it on the dough and cut a circle out; then add one tablespoon of the meat mixture in the center of the dough.
- Then fold the dough over the meat mixture and pinch the edges together using a fork so the filling is sealed. Repeat the above steps until out of dough or meat mixture.
- In a separate bowl, mix some egg white and brush the exterior of the meat pies before baking.
- Arrange meat pies on a baking tray (spray or grease the tray).
- Bake at 350 degrees F for 25 minutes or until brown or golden brown.
- Serve hot or cool.

Ọjọjọ (Water-Yam Fritters)

Serves many

1 large African water-yam - Peel skin and grate

1 red bell pepper - chopped

1 medium onion - chopped

1-2 hot chili pepper - chopped (hot, adjust to taste)

2 -3 maggi or knorr cubes - crushed

Oil or African palm oil - to fry

Salt to taste

PREPARATION

- Peel the skin off the water-yam and grate into a mixing bowl.
- Add chopped red bell pepper, onion, pepper, crushed maggi or knorr, and salt to taste.
- Mix thoroughly.

- **Frying:**
- Deep-fry the mixture by scooping a little amount individually into hot oil and fry until golden. Scoop as many as the frying pan will take. Continue the process until finish.
- Drain on absorbent paper towel in a strainer to remove excess oil.
- Serve hot.

Nigerian Coconut Candy

Serves Many

1 head Fresh Coconut

Coconut Juice - from the coconut

1 cup Sugar - adjust to taste

Water

½ teaspoon salt

PREPARATION

- Break the coconut - Collect the coconut juice.
- Remove the flesh from the shells and cut into tiny pieces. The best way to cut the coconut flesh: slice into thin strips first, then stack few pieces together and chop across in tiny pieces. Continue the process until finish.
- Wash and rinse cut coconut; pour into a medium deep cooking pot; add coconut juice and about half cup of water, salt and sugar and cook at medium high on the stove.
- Once the coconut starts boiling, stir regularly until all the water is just about evaporated.
- Reduce heat to low and continue cooking and stirring. The coconut will start turning brown and sticking together (this is the sugar caramelizing). If it looks drying out before caramelizing takes place, add water little by little and continue stirring.
- Coconut is done when it completely golden in color.
- Turn off the heat and scoop candy onto a flat plate and leave to cool down. Serve or wrap the coconut candy in aluminum foil individually and serve.

Puff-Puff (Nigerian Donuts)

Serves 25 and up

½ bag 5 lbs. All-purpose flour

2 cups of sugar or adjust to taste

2 sachets quick-rising yeast

1 tsp. salt

7-8 cups of very warm water

PREPARATION

- In a large bowl, combine flour, sugar, yeast, salt and mix.
- Pour hot water slowly and mix until desire softness or thickness and lumps free with hand.
- Cover mixed batter and set aside to rise for about three to four hours in a warm or hot spot in the house or outside in the sun. Batter can be mixed and set aside to rise over night also.

Frying:
- Pour oil into a deep fryer and heat. Test the oil by dropping a little batter into the hot oil; batter should float to the top.
- Use a scooper, 1/8 of a cup size, or 1/4 of a cup size to scoop up the batter and gently drop into the hot oil. It will form a ball.
- Also batter can be scooped up by forming a scoop with your hand and scoop up the batter and gently drop into the hot oil. Please be careful with this method.
- Deep fry until light brown or golden brown. Continue this process until the batter is finished.
- Optional: Sprinkle puff-puff with powdered sugar.

Serve hot. Okay to warm in the microwave oven.

Sausage Rolls

Make about 8 (depends on the size)

1 ib. Turkey sausage or sausage of choice

1 small onion – finely chopped

1 large carrot – peeled and grated

Some ginger to taste

Some garlic to taste

2 medium eggs

Some milk to brush the sausage roll

½ tsp. ground black pepper

1-2 maggi or knorr cubes

PREPARATION

- Combine sausage, onion, carrot, ginger, garlic, black pepper, maggi cubes and eggs in a large bowl and mix thoroughly.
- Divide sausage mixture into four (4) and roll out to about four (4) inches long each.
- To make dough see (Meat Pie section) or use readymade dough from store.
- Place rolled sausage on one end edge of dough and roll up to enclose mixture; then cut into 2 pieces each.
- Arrange sausage rolls on a tray (oil the tray first); place seam side down.
- Brush sausage rolls top with milk.
- Bake for 20 – 25 minutes or until golden brown at 350 degree F.
- Cool and serve.

Scotch Eggs

Serves 6

1 dozen eggs

2 - 3lbs. Turkey, chicken, or regular sausage

Breadcrumbs to coat - Finely crushed and seasoned

Flour to coat – Seasoned

4 knorr or maggi cubes - crushed

Ground red pepper to taste - optional

Salt to taste

Oil for frying

PREPARATION

- Boil 6 eggs. Set aside to cool down completely and peel.
- If frozen sausage is used, thaw completely at room temperature.
- Combine the sausage meat with crushed maggi or knorr cubes and mix thoroughly in a bowl.
- Mold sausage meat mixture around the outer layer of each cooked egg one by one.
- In a separate bowl, mix three (3) eggs. Use more eggs if needed.
- In separate bowls, mix breadcrumbs and flour with some pepper and salt for seasoning.
- Dip each molded egg in the beaten eggs; then roll in the breadcrumbs; then in the flour, if necessary dip back in the mix egg and then in the breadcrumbs once more.
- Deep fry eggs in hot oil until golden and crisp and the sausage meat is completely cooked. Carefully remove scotch eggs from the hot oil and drain on absorbent paper towel in the strainer.
- Be careful with hot oil. Do not leave unattended.

Serve whole or slice each one in half for appetizer or as snack.

Spicy Fried Plantains

Serves 4-6

6 ripe Plantains

3 tbsp. of ground ginger or fresh ginger

1 medium onion

2 habaneras pepper (hot adjust to taste)

3 clove garlic

2 knorr or maggi cubes

Water

Oil for frying

PREPARATION

Blend ginger, onion, garlic, pepper, maggi or knorr cubes and water to form a thick paste.

Peel and slice the plantains.

Then, pour the spicy mixture on the plantain and mix well to coat the plantains.

Heating the oil in a skillet and fry the plantain until each side is brown or golden brown.

Remove and place in a paper towel to absorb the excess oil.

Serve hot.

Suya – Nigerian Shish Kabob

Serves many

2 lbs. lean cut beef
2 cups unsalted peanuts - Grind into powder with coffee grinder or mortar and pestle
½ tablespoon hot dry red pepper (adjust to taste)
1 teaspoon ground ginger
1 sweet onion - sliced
3-4 knorr or maggi cubes – crushed
Salt as needed

PREPARATION

- Wash and dry the beef; then slice very thin; skewed into metal or stick skewers and set aside.
- Combine ground peanut, crushed knorr, pepper and ginger and mix thoroughly. Divide into two (2) separate bowls.
- Coat skewed beef with half of the peanuts mixture and marinated for 1-2 hours in the fridge.
- Cooking the suya: place the suya on a hot grill and grill slowly until meat is well done; remove from the grill.
- Sprinkle Suya with the rest of the peanuts mixture all over; top with the sliced onion and serve.

SUBSTITUTION:

Goat meat in place of the beef.

You can cook the Suya in an oven at 350-400 degrees but don't overcook or the meat will dry out.

Now that you have seen a sneak preview of popular Nigerian recipes, please go ahead and try some. They are all easy.

Happy Experimenting!

Appendix A

Kitchen and Household Measurements

1 pinch ………………………....…….. 1/8 tea spoon or less

3 tea spoons………………….….…... 1 table spoon

2 table spoons………………………...……. 1/8 cup

4 table spoons…………………....…………..1/4 cup

8 table spoons……………………….…………..1/2 cup

12 table spoons………………………………….3/4 cup

16 table spoons……………………………... 1 cup

5 table spoons + 1 tea spoon………………...……. 1/3 cup

4 oz…….…………………….………….... 1/2 cup

8oz……………………………………….. ..... 1 cup

16 oz …………………………………..……. 1 lb

1 oz………………………….2 table spoons fat or liquid

1 cup of liquid………………………...…………..1/2 pint

2 cups……………………………….……... 1 pint

2 pints……………………………………. 1 quart

4 cup of liquid……………………………….1 quart

4 quarts…..………………….………….... 1 gallon

8 quarts…..……….......... 1 peck (such as apples, pears, etc.)

1 jigger………………...……………….1 ½ fluid oz

1 jigger………………...….…………….. .3 table spoons

Appendix B
Metric Conversion Table

Kilometers	Miles	Miles	Kilometers
1	0.6	1	1.6
5	3.1	5	8.05
10	6.2	10	16.0
20	12.4	20	32.1
30	18.6	30	48.2
40	24.8	40	64.3
50	31.1	50	80.5
60	37.3	60	96.6
70	43.5	70	112.7
80	49.7	80	128.7
90	55.9	90	144.8
100	62.1	100	160.9
500	310.7	500	804.7
1,000	621.4	1,000	1609.3

CAPACITY		AREA	
10 milliliters	= 1 centiliter	100 sq. millimeters	= 1 sq. centimeter
10 centiliters	= 1 deciliter	100 sq. centimeters	= 1 sq. decimeter
10 deciliters	= 1 liter	100 sq. decimeters	= 1 sq. meter (centare)
10 liters	= 1 dekaliter	100 sq. meters	= 1 are
10 dekaliters	= 1 hectoliter	10,000 sq. meters	= 1 hectare
1,000 liters	= 1 kiloliter (stere)	100 hectares	= 1 sq. kilometer

LENGTH		WEIGHT	
10 millimeters	= 1 centimeter (cm)	10 milligrams	= 1 centigram
10 centimeters	= 1 decimeter	10 centigrams	= 1 decigram
10 decimeters	= 1 meter (m)	10 decigrams	= 1 gram
10 meters	= 1 dekameter	1,000 grams	= 1 kilogram (kilo)
100 meters	= 1 hectometer	100 kilograms	= 1 quintal
1,000 meters	= 1 kilometer	1,000 kilograms	= 1 metric ton

METRIC EQUIVALENT OF U.S. WEIGHTS AND MEASURES			
DRY MEASURE		LONG MEASURE	
1 Pint	= .550599 liter	1 inch	= 2.54 centimeters
1 quart	= 1.101197 liters	1 yard	= .914401 meter
1 peck	= 8.80958 liters	1 mile	= 1.609347 km
1 bushed	= .35238 hectoliter		

LIQUID MEASURE		SQUARE MEASURE	
		1 sq. inch	6.4516 sq. centimeters
1 Pint	= .473167 liter	1 sq. foot	9.29034 sq. decimeters
1 quart	= .946332 liter	1 sq. yard	.836131 sq. meter
1 gallon	= 3.785329 liters	1 acre	.40469 hectares
		1 sq. mile	2.59 sq. kilometers (259 hectares)

AVOIRDUPOIS MEASURE		CUBIC MEASURE	
1 ounce	= 28.349527 grams	1 cu. Inch	= 16.3872 cu. Centimeters
1 pound	= .453592 kilograms	1 cu. Foot	= .028317 cu. Meter
1 short ton	= .90718486 metric ton	1 cu. yard	= .76456 cu meter
1 long ton	= 1.01604704 metric tons		

Appendix C
About Some Nigerian Ingredients

Most of the ingredients used in this web site can be obtained in supermarkets although some items may only be found in African food shops. Where this is not available I have recommended alternative ingredients that can be used to achieve almost the same results.

- **Afang / Ukazi leaves (gnetum African)**
  Dark green Shiny foliage of the creeping afang plant cultivated mostly in Calabar and Igbo land are used a great deal in the cooking of these regions. It can be bought ready shredded from African food stores.

- **Atama leaves/Beletientien**
  This is an annual Herb cultivated in the delta areas. It smells and taste like tarragon; usually used fresh or dried in Banga soup. Use dried leaves sparingly as flavor is more intense. Readily available from African food stores.

- **Avocado (persea Americana)**
  Tropical fruit with thick warty skin usually greenish or purplish in color. The edible flesh inside surrounds a large oval shape seed. It is light yellow and soft when ripe. Avocados can be eaten on its own or cut in half and filled with cooked seafood (Avocado and prawn cocktail).

- **Beans or Cowpeas**
  Black-eye beans or Brown beans have become indispensable in Nigeria cuisine because of it versatility in use.

- **Banana**
  This is one of the most important food crops in Nigeria. Widely eaten on it's own or in fruit salads they make a good substitute for plantains. The leaves are usually used for wrapping foods such as Anyan-Ekpang or Ebiripo for steaming. Baking foil or greased parchment paper make adequate substitute but do not add the delicate flavour that banana leaves give.

- **Bitterleaf**
  A leafy green vegetable that is widely used in soups like Egusi for its bitter but sweet flavor. The fresh leaves is prepared like spinach and washed with salt; rubbing and

squeezing to remove some of the bitterness before use. Can be bought fresh or ready washed and air-dried.

- **Chilli Peppers**
  Chilli peppers are the fruit of Capsicum Frutescens plant with red orange or yellow pods which are very hot rich in Vitamin A & C and widely used in Nigerian cooking. While the flavor in the chilli lies in the flesh and skins much of the heat potency rests in the seeds and veins which can be removed. Green chillies are a lot hotter than the red ones. The active chemical con stituent is capiasin renowned for stimulating digestive process and helping to relieve heat fatigue in hot climates by inducing perspiration.

- **Breadfruit**
  These are large green fruits which hang like lanterns from tress. Only edible when cooked and taste like boiled potatoes. It could also be fried as crisp.

- **Cassava (Manihot esculenta)**
  Cassava is a tropical vegetable with a long tu berous root and dull green palmate leaves. Mature tubers have brown mottled skin with a white fibrous flesh. It can be cooked and eaten with coconut (Eberebe); but mostly used for making Gari (Cassava grains) and Fufu. Used as accompaniment to soups and stews. It can be bought ready-made as gaff or cassava flour (Fufu).

- **Cocoyam**
  Cocoyams are similar to large potatoes usually with a fibrous skin. In Nigeria the plant is grown for both its tubers and leaves. The young and tender leaves are used in preparing Ekpang Nkukwo (cocoa-yam pottage). Spinach leaves make adequate substitute. These tubers can also be boiled roasted or fried.

- **Corn/Maize**
  Sweet corn or maize as it is commonly known is grown throughout Nigeria as a food source. The plant grows to a height of about seven feet. When fully mature, the swollen fruits are called cobs and it is these, which are picked and used for food. The cobs can be boiled, roasted, or cooked with beans as a main course. A number of by products are obtained from the grains including ogi (corn-starch) and corn oil, which is low in saturates and cholesterol.

- **Crayfish**
  Smoked dried prawns or shrips used for flavoring soups and savory dishes. Usually whole or ground.

- **Egusi (cirullus colocynthis) melon seeds**
  Seed of the African melon fruit used in preparing Egusi soup. Should be grinded before use. Can be oily but adds a nutty flavor to the soup.

- **Ewedu (corchorus olitorius)**
  Shiny green leave vegetable rich in Vitamins A C & D. Use in making sauces to accompany stews and enjoyed for its mucilaginous or viscous properties. Sold fresh or dried.

- **Elubo**
  Dried powdered yam flour for making amala (cooked yam flour pudding).

- **Fufu**
  Fermented cassava dough usually served cooked to accompany soups

- **Garden eggs (solanum melongena)**
  Also knows as African eggplant a member of the aubergine family. A round shiny green and yel low fruit with a slightly bitter taste. Garden eggs are eaten raw as a fruit or diced and added to stews.

- **Groundnut (Arachis hypogaea)**
  Like a set of twins groundnut mature together in light coloured shells which are flaky and easy to break. Grown profusely in Northern Nigeria the seeds are harvested for their oil and protein. They can be eaten raw boiled roasted and pureed for making groundnut soup. Groundnut oil is used for cooking.

- **Iru (locust bean) parkia biglobosa**
  Fermented locust or black beans. They have a slightly salty taste and a pungent smell. They are used as seasoning in soups. Usually sold fresh or dried packed.

- **Kaun (Rock salt) potash**
  Usually added to food especially pulses during cooking for faster tenderisation and to increase the viscosity In Okro and Ewedu sauce. Also used for emulsifying oil and water in some traditional soups.

- **Mango (mangifera indica)**
  This kidney shaped fruit is pinkish or yellowish in colour. When fully ripe it is lusciously sweet and succulent with the golden flesh. Mango is common in fruit platters and salad.

- **Millet (pennisetum)**
  Tiny yellow grains obtained from plant that looks like bull rushes with a maize like stalk. Grows widely in Northern Nigeria and used mostly for porridge and gruel.

- **Okra (lady fingers)**
  These vegetables are curved seed pod up to 9 inches Long they are usually eaten cooked in soup and salads.

- **Apon (ogbono Seed)**
  This seeds are obtained from the nuts of the African oro fruit and air dried in the sun. It has a subtle aromatic flavor and it's very mucilaginous when cooked. Can be bought whole or powdered.

- **Pawpaw (Carica papaya)**
  This is a fruit of woody herbaceous plant that looks like a tree. It is eaten ripe (yellow or orange in color) in fruit salads or stuffed for starters or main course.

- **Plantain**
  A large member of the banana family plantain is less sweet than banana and is more versatile in use. It is often boiled toasted or fried and served with meat stews because the tissue has a starchy taste than sweet banana. It is best cooked with plenty of spices onions tomatoes and peppers (plantain pottage).

- **Ugwu (Pumpkin leaves) telfairi occidentallis**
  These trailing green leaves of the pumpkin plant rich in minerals and vitamins. Use in various soup preparations It is the chief ingredient in cooking Edikang Ikong soup. Fresh spinach can be used as substitute in any recipe if not available. Pumpkin seeds can also be eaten.

- **Utazi leaves (crongromena ratifolia)**
  This is a bitter tasting pale green leaf usually used for flavouring pepper soup. Very sparingly used. It can also be used as a substitute for bitter leaves.

- **Uzouza leaves or Ikong Etinkinrin**
  This sweet smelling aromatic and spicy pale green leaf vegetable is also used for flavoring soups especially (Ibaba soup).

- **Yam (Dioscorea sp)**
  The plant grows as a vine to height of six to eight feet. The edible tubers comes in various

shapes and sizes; usually dark brown in color and hairy to the touch. The flesh is white or yellow and when cooked it has a pleasant flavor when cooked rather like potato. It is harvested in dry season with a gig feast known as Yam Festival in Igbo land. Yam still forms the staple diet of a large number of people in Nigeria. It is cooked in different ways including boiled roasted and fried. When pounded it is served as accompaniment to soups and stews.

- **Sorghum**
  Also known as guinea corn sorghum is cultivated mainly in Northern Nigeria. Used for porridge or pap (gruel).

- **Snail**
  These are large forest creatures covered with a hard shell. Taste rubbery when overcooked it is rather an acquired taste.

- **Oils**
  From a health stand point fats and oils are either saturated or unsaturated. Saturated oils such as butter coconut and palm oil are known to increase the amount of cholesterol carried in the blood but since regional cuisine is characterized by the type of oil used lesser quantities or half the amount in a given recipe could always be used.

- **Groundnut oil**
  This is used for frying and also added to stews and other savory dishes. It has a pleasant and unobtrusive taste; favorable in making mayonnaise and could be heated to a high temperature without burning.

- **Corn oil**
  This oil pressed from the germ of germ of maize (corn) is high in poly unsaturated and low in cholesterol. It is used the same way as groundnut oil. It can also be heated to a high temperature without burning.

- **Palm oil**
  This rather tasty and nutty thick and waxy rustic red colored oil is extracted from the flesh of the oil-palm nut fruits. It is widely used in Nigerian cooking especially in the traditional soups and stews for color and taste but usually in small quantity as it is high in saturates.

- **Water leaf (talilum triangulare)**
  This is the most widely used of all green leaf vegetables. It is rich in iron calcium and

vitamin A and C and it is best eaten lightly cooked in soups and stews. spinach can be used in recipes calling for waterleaf.

- **Kuka leaves**
  Leaves of the baobab tree usually sold dried in powder form and used for Kuka soup.

- **IGBO (garden egg leaves) solanum manocarpum**
  The young leaves of the garden eggplant. African Aubergines can be eaten raw in salads or cooked in stews.

- **Soko (celosia argentea)**
  This green leaf vegetable is much preferred in the making of Efo-riro. It taste like spinach.

- **Tete (celosia viddis)**
  This green is a close relative to Soko and is used interchangeable or in combination with it. It is widely grown in Western Nigeria.

Appendix D
Uses of Vinegar in the Kitchen

➢ A mixture of salt and vinegar will clean coffee and tea stains from chinaware.

➢ Freshen vegetables. Soak wilted vegetables in 2 cups of water and a tablespoon of vinegar.

➢ Boil better eggs by adding 2 tablespoons to water before boiling. Keeps them from cracking.

➢ Marinating meat in vinegar kills bacteria and tenderizes the meat. Use one-quarter cup vinegar for a two to three pound roast, marinate overnight, and then cook without draining or rinsing the meat.

➢ Add herbs to the vinegar when marinating as desired.

➢ Put vinegar on a cloth and let sit on the back of your kitchen faucet and it removes hard water stains.

➢ Vinegar can help to dissolve mineral deposits that collect in automatic drip coffee makers. Fill the reservoir with vinegar and run it through a brewing cycle. Rinse thoroughly with water when the cycle is finished. (Be sure to check the owner's manual for specific instructions).

➢ Brass, copper and pewter will shine if cleaned with the following mixture. Dissolve 1 teaspoon of salt in one (1) cup of distilled vinegar.

➢ Clean the dishwasher by running a cup of vinegar through the whole cycle once a month to reduce soap build up on the inner mechanisms and on glassware.

➢ Deodorize the kitchen drain. Pour a cup of vinegar down the drain once a week. Let stand 30 minutes and then flush with cold water.

➢ Unclog a drain. Pour a handful of baking soda down the drain and add ½ cup of vinegar. Rinse with hot water.

➢ Eliminate onion odor by rubbing vinegar on your fingers before and after slicing.

➢ Clean and disinfect wood cutting boards by wiping with full strength vinegar.

➢ Cut grease and odor on dishes by adding a tablespoon of vinegar to hot soapy water.

➢ Clean a teapot by boiling a mixture of water and vinegar in it. Wipe away the grime.

➢ Clean and deodorize the garbage disposal by making vinegar ice cubes and feed them down the disposal. After grinding, run cold water through.

- Clean and deodorize jars. Rinse mayonnaise, peanut butter, and mustard jars with vinegar when empty.
- Get rid of cooking smells by letting a small pot of vinegar and water simmer on the stove.
- Clean the refrigerator by washing with a solution of equal parts water and vinegar.
- Clean stainless steel by wiping with vinegar dampened cloth.
- Clean china and fine glassware by adding a cup of vinegar to a sink of warm water. Gently dip the glass or china in the solution and let dry.
- Get stains out of pots by filling the pots with a solution of three (3) tablespoons of vinegar to a pint of water. Boil until stain loosens and can be washed away.
- Clean food-stained pots and pans by filling the pots and pans with vinegar and let stand for thirty minutes. Then rinse in hot, soapy water.
- Clean the microwave by boiling a solution of ¼ cup of vinegar and 1 cup of water in the microwave. It will loosen splattered on food and deodorize.
- Make buttermilk. Add a tablespoon of vinegar to a cup of milk and let it stand for five (5) minutes to thicken.
- Replace a lemon by substituting ¼ teaspoon of vinegar for 1 teaspoon of lemon juice.
- Firm up gelatin by adding a teaspoon of vinegar for every box of gelatin used. To keep those molded desserts from sagging in the summer heat.
- Prepare fluffier rice by adding a teaspoon of vinegar to the water when it boils.
- Make wine vinegar by mixing two (2) tablespoons of vinegar with 1 teaspoon of dry red wine.
- Debug fresh vegetables by washing them in water with vinegar and salt. Bugs float off.
- Scale fish more easily by rubbing with vinegar five (5) minutes before scaling.
- Prevent soap film on glassware by placing a cup of vinegar on the bottom rack of your dishwasher, run for five minutes, then run though the full cycle.
- The minerals found in foods and water will often leave a dark stain on aluminum utensils. This stain can be easily removed by boiling a solution of 1 tablespoon of distilled vinegar per cup of water in the utensil. Utensils may also be boiled in the solution.
- Unsightly film in small-necked bottles and other containers can be cleaned by pouring vinegar into the bottle and shaking. For tougher stains, add a few tablespoons of rice

or sand and shake vigorously. Rinse thoroughly and repeat until clean or determined hopeless.

➢ After cleaning the bread box, keep it smelling sweet by wiping it down with a cloth moistened in distilled vinegar.

➢ To eliminate fruit stains from your hands, rub your hands with a little distilled vinegar and wipe with a cloth

➢ Grease build-up in an oven can be prevented by wiping with a cleaning ran that has been moistened in distilled vinegar and water.

➢ Formica tops and counters will shine in cleaned with a cloth soaked in distilled vinegar.

➢ No-wax linoleum will shine better if wiped with a solution of ½ cup of white vinegar in ½ gallon of water.

➢ Stains on hard-to-clean glass, aluminum, or porcelain utensils may be loosened by boiling in a solution of one part vinegar to eight parts water. The utensils should then be washed in hot soapy water.

Appendix E
Useful Kitchen Tips

Ginger Therapy

➤ Ginger up! Ginger can spice up a lot of things with ginger. Ginger is a multi-faceted root not only for cooking, but also for therapeutic applications in the home. Two common applications are for cough/sore throat therapy and relief of indigestion.

➤ Directions: Scrape off the bark from the root, and cut the remaining root into small, cough-drop-sized pieces. The taste is very strong, and has a spicy flavor. For mild relief, suck the ginger for a light dose of the juice, and for more intensity, bite slightly into the root to squeeze more of the juice out. This is very effective if you feel you are about to cough.

➤ Ginger also acts as a digestive aid. It can cut through excess mucous, and help relieve an upset stomach. Chew up on the cough-drop ginger pieces and swallow them to relieve indigestion. There is a ginger tea that helps with this, with colds, and with coughing.

➤ Making Ginger Tea: To make ginger tea, prepare the root the same way it is done for cough drops. Cut the ginger into chunks, and put in a saucepan with a good quantity of filtered or spring water. Slowly cook the brew until about three quarters of the water boils off. This will produce a very spicy tea, which will aid the digestion and even help strengthen the immune system.

Uses of baking soda in the kitchen

Baking soda is a chemical compound, bicarbonate of soda, that appears as a fine powder. It releases bubbles of carbon dioxide when it interacts with an acid and a liquid. It is most commonly used in baking, where it acts as a leavening agent. It has many different uses in the kitchen. It often works better than many commercially available and expensive products for the same uses.

➤ Sprinkle baking soda on grease or electrical fire to safely put it out. This also works for car engine fire. Baking soda will also put out fires in clothing, fuel, wood, upholstery and rugs.

➤ Clean vegetables and fruit with baking soda. Sprinkle in water, soak and rinse the vegetables.

➤ Wash garbage cans with baking soda to freshen and eliminate odors.

- Oil and grease in clothes stains will wash out better with soda added to the washing water.
- Clean fridge and freezer with dry baking soda sprinkled on a damp cloth and rinse with clear water.
- Deodorize fridge and freezer by putting in an open container of baking soda to absorb odors. Stir and turn over the soda from time to time. Replace every 2 months.
- Wash food and drink containers with baking soda and water.
- Wash marble-topped kitchen cabinet furniture with a solution of three tablespoons of baking soda in one quart of warm water. Let stand awhile and then rinse with clear water.
- Wash out thermos bottles and cooling containers with soda and water to get rid of stale smells.
- To remove stubborn stains from marble or plastic surfaces, scour with a paste of soda and water.
- Wash glass or stainless steel coffee pots (but not aluminum) in a soda solution (three teaspoons of soda to one quart water).
- For better cleaning of coffee maker, run it through its cycle with baking soda solution and rinse clean.
- Give baby bottles a good cleaning with soda and hot water.
- Sprinkle soda on barbecue grills, let soak, and then rinse off.
- Polish silverware with dry soda on a damp cloth. Rub, rinse, and dry.
- Reduce odor build-up in dishwasher by sprinkling some baking soda on the bottom.
- Run dishwasher through its cycle with baking soda in it instead of soap to give it a good cleaning.
- To remove burned-on food from a pan, let the pan soak in baking soda and water for ten minutes before washing. Alternately, scrub the pot with dry baking soda and a moist scouring pad.
- For a badly-burned pan with a thick layer of burned-on food, pour a thick layer of baking soda directly onto the bottom of the pan. Then sprinkle on just enough water so as to moisten the soda. Leave the pot overnight. Scrub it clean next day.
- Rub stainless steel and chrome with a moist cloth and dry baking soda to shine it up. Rinse and dry. On stainless steel, scrub in the Directions of the grain.

- ➤ Clean plastic, porcelain and glass with dry baking soda on a damp cloth. Rinse and dry.

- ➤ Keep drains clean and free-flowing by putting four tablespoons of soda in them each week. Flush the soda down with hot water.

- ➤ To remove strong odors from hands, wet hands and rub them hard with baking soda, then rinse.

- ➤ Sprinkle baking soda on wet toothbrush and brush teeth and dentures with it.

- ➤ Apply soda directly to insect bites, rashes, and poison ivy to relieve discomfort. Make a paste with water.

- ➤ For plucking chickens, add one teaspoon of baking soda to the boiling water. The feathers will come off easier and flesh will be clean and white.

- ➤ Add to water to soak dried beans to make them more digestible.

- ➤ Use to remove melted plastic bread wrapper from toaster, dampen cloth and make a mild abrasive with baking soda.

Uses of lemon juice in the kitchen

"A little lemon juice makes everything taste better." – Virginia Sanborn Burleigh

Lemons originated in India and have been used for trading purposes for centuries. Lemons were originally called "the golden apples." This inexpensive fruit is very useful and versatile.

- ➤ To make substitute buttermilk, mix one cup of milk with a tablespoon of lemon juice for a buttermilk substitute that works great!

- ➤ To sanitize dishwasher and remove mineral deposits and odors, remove all dishes. Place 1/4 cup of lemon juice in the soap dispenser and run through the normal cycle. Dishwasher will be clean and smell wonderful!

- ➤ To clean copper pots, cover the surface of a half lemon with salt and scrub. Rinse and buff with a soft cloth for a beautiful shine.

- ➤ To clean silver, clean with lemon juice and buff with a soft cloth.

- ➤ Lemon juice also cleans the tarnish off brass.

- ➤ To remove the smell of garlic or onions from hands, rub with a lemon slice and rinse.

Uses of honey in the kitchen

Honey is the only food in the world that will not spoil or rot. It will do what some people refer to as "turning to sugar." In reality honey is always honey. However, when left in a cool dark place for a long time it will crystallize.

"You can sweeten two pots with only one drop of honey." – Deji Badiru, June 22, 2010

"You catch more flies with honey than with vinegar." – A Common Saying

Both honey and vinegar have their respective uses in the kitchen. For honey's sake, we list the following kitchen uses:

➢ Tasty additive to foods and drinks
➢ Use as a sugar substitute when cooking or baking
➢ Remedy for diabetic ulcer to speed up the healing process
➢ Relaxant for anxiety and nervousness
➢ Antibacterial solution --- Honey has antibacterial properties due to its acidic nature and produces hydrogen peroxide through an enzymic process
➢ Remedy for burns, particularly as first-aid in kitchen accidents
➢ Treatment for sore throat --- to grease the passage of food on the gastronomic journey
➢ Enhancement to Vitamin A
➢ Immune system and energy booster
➢ Antiseptic
➢ Honey taken with cinnamon powder can ease stomachache
➢ Good antioxidant

When honey jar lid hardens, loosen the lid by boiling some water and sitting the honey Jar in the hot water. Turn off the heat and let the jar content liquefy. It is then as good as before. Never boil honey or put it in a microwave. To do so will kill the enzymes in the honey.

Facts on Honey and Cinnamon:

- ➤ It is found that a mixture of honey and Cinnamon cures most diseases.

- ➤ Honey is produced in most of the countries of the world.

- ➤ Honey can be used without any side effects for any kind of diseases.

- ➤ Even though honey is sweet, if taken in the right dosage as a medicine, it does not harm diabetic patients.

- ➤ For bladder infection, take two tablespoons of cinnamon powder and one teaspoon of honey in a glass of lukewarm water and drink it. It destroys the germs in the bladder.

- ➤ For upset stomach, honey taken with cinnamon powder mitigates stomach ache and also reduces the symptoms of stomach ulcers.

- ➤ Some studies done in India and Japan conjecture that if honey is taken with cinnamon powder, the stomach is relieved of gas.

- ➤ It is believed that cinnamon powder sprinkled on two tablespoons of honey, taken before meal, can relieve acidity to facilitate digestion.